IN ENDLESS MORN OF LIGHT

Borgo Press Books by MICHAEL R. COLLINGS

All Calm, All Bright: Christmas Offerings
The Art and Craft of Poetry: Twenty Exercises Toward Mastery
Brian Aldiss
Dark Transformations: Deadly Visions of Change
The Films of Stephen King
GemLore: An Introduction to Precious and Semi-Precious Gemstones
The House Beyond the Hill: A Novel of Horror
In Endless Morn of Light: Moral Freedom in Milton's Universe
In the Void: Poems of Science Fiction, Myth and Fantasy, & Horror
The Many Facets of Stephen King
Matrix: Echoes of Growing Up West
Naked to the Sun: Dark Visions of Apocalypse
The Nephiad: An Epic Poem in XII Books
Piers Anthony
Scaring Us to Death: The Impact of Stephen King on Popular Culture
Singer of Lies: A Science Fantasy Novel
Tales Through Time: Poems, Revised and Enlarged Edition
Toward Other Worlds: Perspectives on John Milton, C. S. Lewis, Stephen King, Orson Scott Card, and Others
Wer Means Man, and Other Tales of Terror and Wonder
Wordsmith, Part One: The Veil of Heaven: A Science Fantasy Novel
Wordsmith, Part Two: The Thousand Eyes of Flame: A Science Fantasy Novel

IN ENDLESS MORN OF LIGHT

MORAL FREEDOM IN MILTON'S UNIVERSE

by

Michael R. Collings

Emeritus Professor of English
Seaver College
Pepperdine University

THE BORGO PRESS

An Imprint of Wildside Press LLC

MMX

The Milford Series
Popular Writers of Today
ISSN 0163-2469

Volume Fourteen

Copyright © 2010 by Michael R. Collings

All rights reserved.
No part of this book may be reproduced in any form
without the expressed written consent
of the author and publisher.
Printed in the United States of America.

www.wildsidebooks.com

FIRST EDITION

CONTENTS

Introduction 7
Acknowledgments 12
Further Acknowledgments .... .13
Abbreviations 14

CHAPTER I: Milton and Moral Liberty—Some Christian and Classical Sources 15

CHAPTER II: Toward a Definition of Liberty—the Early Poetry and the Prose 44
  i. The Early Minor Poems 44
  ii. Comus 54
  iii. Lycidas 65
  iv. The Prose 71
  v. Summation 75

CHAPTER III: The Father—Fountainhead of Moral Freedom 79

CHAPTER IV: The Son—Paradigm of Righteous Choice 92
  i. The Nature of the Son 92
  ii. The Early Poems 100
  iii. The Epics 107

CHAPTER V: The First Levels of Creation—The Material Universe and the Angels 119
  i. The Material Universe 119
  ii. Unfallen Angels 127

    iii. Satan and the Fallen Angels 136

CHAPTER VI: Man in Eden—Choice and Consequence 152
    i. Man's Responsibility for Sin 152
    ii. Adam and Eve in the Garden............................ 157
    iii. The Fall.. 163
    iv. After the Fall 171

CHAPTER VII: Man's Freedom of Choice and the Return to God
.... 175
    i. Fallen Man in a Fallen World 175
    ii. The Destiny of Man 187

EPILOGUE 198

Bibliography of Works Cited and Consulted.............................. 200
Index 206
About the Author 215

INTRODUCTION

Much criticism has responded to the complexities of Milton's genius by assigning him to various—and often contradictory—schools of belief. Even a brief survey of scholarship demonstrates that such discussions of his theology rarely share any overriding consensus. Milton appears orthodox to one critic, heterodox to another, and heretical to yet another. He is an adoptive classicist, a humanist, a Calvinist, a Puritan, an apocalyptic reformer, a traditionalist, and, to some, even a Catholic. He is an optimistic idealist and a pessimistic pragmatist, an Arian, a subordinationist, an Arminian, a predestinarian, a Socinian, a Platonist, a mystic, and a rationalist. Given the range of Milton's interests and talents, such widely diverging evaluations are not at all surprising. In fact, Milton's own emphasis on the validity of individual assessment of traditions and truths belies by definition attempts to force him into restrictive categories; and perhaps more crucially, his own beliefs shifted substantially over the years. And yet there is at least one area of near unanimity among scholars. For all of his complexity—and occasional obscurity—Milton clearly identifies himself as a passionate advocate of human liberty.

Milton's career as poet and public figure reflects clearly his interest in the possibilities of human choice. One need only think of the varieties of human alternatives in *Comus,* "L'Allegro," "Il Penseroso," and *Lycidas*, for example, to appreciate the importance of individual decision to Milton's world view. Even after the inception of the struggle between King and Commonwealth, when Milton chose to defer his poetic ambitions and to dedicate his talents to the state, he recounts his service in defending English liberties—

ecclesiastical, domestic, and civil—in the *Second Defense of the English People*.

Studies of Milton's careers as poet and apologist have offered plausible explanations for Milton's beliefs, based on elements in the seventeenth-century milieu. Momentarily setting aside the question of particular identifiable sources, it remains nonetheless true that Milton's belief in the dignity of humans as rational, volitive creatures continues from his earliest works until his last. Even the crushing disappointment and personal defeat accompanying the Restoration failed to stifle completely Milton's confidence in humanity's capacity to determine in some measure its temporal and eternal destiny.

Of course, much of what I have just said is almost a commonplace. A cursory glance at late twentieth-century scholarship indicates the extent to which critics have engaged this element of Milton's poetics and theology. Studies by J. M. Evans, Stella Revard, A. S. P. Woodhouse, Mary Ann Nevins Radzinowicz, Elizabeth Eastland, John E. Seaman, Harry F. Robbins, Lawrence Babb, Michael Fixler, Ruth Bartholomew, Barry Gross, Gary Hamilton, Diane McColley, Herschel Baker, and others have directly confronted manifestations of freedom to choose in the various levels of Milton's universe and have greatly clarified a crucial point in Milton's theology. Yet there is still a need to synthesize the resulting information, to establish patterns by which responsibility and choice interlink and function throughout Milton's poetic universe.

In Milton's prose and poetry, as in his theology, the freedom of choice enjoyed by all rational beings constantly intertwines, creating models of true and false choice upon which subsequent decisions may—and often *must*—be made. The Father's Will and Decrees—themselves both the source and ultimate end of all moral liberty—are the only boundaries externally imposed upon choice in Milton's universe. As rational beings choose righteously or falsely, they themselves either expand the possibilities of choice to the fullest limits (perfect obedience to the will of God) or systematically restrict themselves to the servitude of self-bondage, despair, and ultimately death. Through proper choice, rational beings draw nearer to the Father and participate more fully in His attributes; through improper choice, they re-create the archetypal Fall of Satan, withdrawing from the light and goodness of the Father. This study, then, examines the relationships between rational creatures and the Deity, relationships which are defined by a pervasive and complex web of choices and reciprocal responsibility.

Milton did not, of course, write in a cultural vacuum. Perhaps more than any other major poet, Milton prepared himself for his vocation as epic poet through a lifetime of diligent and exhaustive study. He was familiar with the seminal minds of Christian and classical thought, but even more importantly, he developed a dynamic eclecticism which incorporated into his structure of truth fragments from widely diverging sources. Hence his conceptions of the Father and the Son, of humanity and angels, and of the universe itself draw upon Church Fathers, pagan philosophical speculation, contemporary thought and belief, and his own sense of personal inspiration. Chapter I of this study summarizes some of the more influential backgrounds and traditions available to Milton as he formed his beliefs on the moral agency and inherent dignity of all rational beings. Chapter II shows Milton's attempts in the early prose and poetry to express his growing commitment to the idea of a universe imbued with choice and responsibility.

At the apex of such a universe, of course, stands the Father, and any discussion which purports to define moral freedom must perforce begin with the Father's absolute freedom and goodness. The Father's every creative impulse, from the generation of the Son to the creation of the invisible and visible cosmos, represents not only conscious freedom of choice (since otherwise the Father would be limited by and subject to a superior will, a possibility which Milton would strenuously deny), but also an extension of that freedom to increasingly distant levels of rational beings. Chapters III and IV discuss the Father's absolute decrees concerning the freedom of His creatures and that freedom as exemplified by the Son, the paradigm of righteous adherence to the Father's will.

The Father's creation of the material universe and the angels endows the angels with the freedom of choice enjoyed by the Father and the Son, but for the first time, false choice enters the universe. Chapter V examines the varied responses of loyal and disloyal angels to the possibilities of choice in Heaven and Hell. By following the lead of Christ and conforming freely to the Father's will, the loyal angels paradoxically expand and perfect their freedom of choice; by rejecting righteous alternatives in favor of self-directed license, Satan and the rebel angels commit themselves to the absolute bondage of an external and an internal Hell. Their apparently unrestricted freedom of choice is in fact total bondage to self, sin, and darkness.

The reactions to the Father's decree of free choice among His creatures provide an additional pattern of proper and improper choice for the Father's final creation—Adam and Eve and their progeny. Chapter VI investigates Milton's evidences for the first human couple's primary responsibility for their fall into mortality. They are formed perfect, though mutable; they are instructed by angelic messengers and revelatory dreams, and given sufficient knowledge of both righteous choice and perverted license to recognize and avoid evil. As rational creatures, they are implicitly capable of withstanding any overt advances of evil, drawing support from the righteous pattern of obedience offered by the Son and the loyal angels; yet through mischoice, they freely descend into enslavement by self, sin, and death. The choice to fall is theirs alone.

The Father, the Son, and the angels loyal and rebellious do not remake choices, since they either have no need or no power to do so. Of all rational beings, only human beings remain in flux. Since their fall was in part external (although ultimately the result of conscious decisions), they are granted the mercy denied to Satan and the rebels. Accordingly, Chapter VII traces the stages by which Adam and Eve and their posterity avail themselves of the promised redemption which faith and obedience make possible. Through the mediation of the Son, each individual may be reunited with God.

Thus Milton brings freedom of choice full circle, returning through repentant humanity to Christ and to the Father, whence true liberty springs. The Father is not lessened as He allows His creatures the opportunity to choose for themselves obedience or rebellion, sanctification through Christ or debasement with Satan. Instead, He is magnified by the righteous worship of creatures conforming to His will through love and voluntary obedience, while those who have cut themselves off from the goodness of the Father become unknowing and unwitting tools by which He brings forth good out of evil.

Freedom of choice, then, is not merely a poetic device or didactic embellishment imposed upon Milton's writings. It is instead a crucial key to understanding the motives and actions of rational beings on all levels of existence. Milton's unyielding faith in the freedom of choice which characterizes all rational beings—celestial, angelic, and human—allows him to create in his prose and poetry the image of a universe which is unified and ultimately harmonious.

ACKNOWLEDGMENTS

Much like Milton's "Subject for Heroic Song," the subject for this study "Pleas'd me long choosing, and beginning late...." The conclusions arrived at in this study grew out of Dr. William Geiger's undergraduate courses at Whittier College and Dr. John M. Steadman's graduate seminars at the University of California, Riverside. I am deeply indebted to both men for their unflagging enthusiasm for Milton, an enthusiasm at once refreshing and contagious. I also wish to acknowledge the aid and advice of the members of my dissertation committee: Dr. Steadman, who devoted much time and effort to suggesting improvements; Dr. Catherine Shaw; and Dr. Milton Miller. And finally, I am grateful to my family for their support during the past two years: to Judith for her patience as a dissertation-widow; and to Michael Brent, Erika, and Ethan for providing me with much-needed diversion.

Michael R. Collings
University of California, Riverside
June, 1977

FURTHER ACKNOWLEDGMENTS

In the intervening four decades since this study was first attempted, much has changed, in the world, in academia, in Milton studies, in attitudes toward literature and literary criticism, and not the least in my own circumstances. To the list of those who deserve my gratitude must be add Kendra, as well as in-laws and grandchildren who reside never far from my mind. And to my awareness of and interest in Milton must be added my years of teaching literature and composition at Pepperdine University, including many classes in Sixteenth- and Seventeenth-Century literature; copious reading in the history and religious fervor that paralleled Milton's life; and my own essay into the practice of epic theory, resulting in *The Nephiad*, begun while I was under the tutelage of John Steadman at the University of California, Riverside, and completed twenty-five years later while I served as Director of Creative Writing and Professor of English at Pepperdine. The 6,500+ lines of that poem afforded me the uncommon opportunity to put Milton's poetics into practice and led, I think, to a deeper understanding of *Paradise Lost* and the workings of Milton's mind.

As before, my deepest thanks go to Dr. Geiger and Dr. Steadman who, after forty years, still stand as models of Renaissance gentlemen and true scholars. To Judi for constant support and encouragement. And to my family, however far scattered.

Michael R. Collings
Meridian, Idaho
Summer 2009

ABBREVIATIONS

CD	*De Doctrina Christiana/The Christian Doctrine*
CPW	*Complete Prose Works of John Milton* (Yale Prose)
PL	*Paradise Lost*
PR	*Paradise Regained*
SA	*Samson Agonistes*

CE	*College English*
ELH	*Journal of English Literary History*
HTR	*Harvard Theological Review*
JHI	*Journal of the History of Ideas*
JWCI	*Journal of the Warburg and Courtauld Institute*
MLN	*Modern Language Notes*
MLQ	*Modern Language Quarterly*
MLR	*Modern Language Review*
MP	*Modern Philology*
MQ	*Milton Quarterly*
MS	*Milton Studies*
PJE	*Peabody Journal of Education*
PMLA	*Publications of the Modern Language Association*
PQ	*Philological Quarterly*
RES	*Review of English Studies*
SAB	*South Atlantic Bulletin*
SEL	*Studies in English Literature*
SP	*Studies in Philology*
SR	*Southwest Review*
UTQ	*University of Toronto Quarterly*

CHAPTER ONE

Milton and Moral Liberty—
Some Christian and Classic Sources

"Theological truth is sunk in a deep well, whence it cannot be drawn without great labour."—Arminius to Johannes Uytenbogaert[1]

No idea is more consistent throughout Milton's writings than his belief in absolute freedom of choice and in the concomitant rights and responsibilities of that freedom. From his earliest writings until the final statements in the great poems of the last decades, Milton continually returns to his belief in the inviolable freedom of men and angels to determine their own actions. The vital role of freedom of choice—including as it does the more technical consideration of Christian liberty, itself a widely debated term ranging from government by the saints to perfection of inward freedom—informs much in Milton's writings. His beliefs may have altered as time and circumstances altered (and many critical studies have probed this process in Milton's development), but he nonetheless consistently advocated liberty and freedom of choice, both internal and external.

Milton's beliefs defy simplistic analyses of sources and influences. His extensive reading enabled him to synthesize elements from disparate philosophies, theologies, and sciences. Consequently, in order to understand the foundations of Milton's belief in freedom, it is often more fruitful to note the broad philosophical and theologi-

---

[1] A. W. Harrison, *Arminianism* (London: Duckworth, 1937), pp. 16-17.

cal supports for self-determination available to him than to seek particular sources.[2]

Milton epitomized the Renaissance "double truth," the apparent conflict between two modes of knowing, the rationality of classical philosophy and the revelation of Christianity. Milton's greatness stems in part from his ability to draw at will from each of these traditions, to employ fragments of each, and yet to hold himself aloof from exclusive adherence to the strictures of either. Certainly the traditional picture of the severe Milton, the narrow, orthodox, archetypal Puritan, is no longer wholly valid, replaced by the larger image of Milton as receptacle for truth in whatever guise or from whatever direction it presented itself to his inquiring mind.

Milton's concern with the freedom or bondage of the human will, like other of his beliefs, was supported by a fusion of several respected and well-documented traditions. The early Greek philosophers were divided on the question; the Eleatics, Democritus, and the Stoics opposed the freedom of the will, while the Pythagoreans, Socrates, Aristotle, and Epicurus defended it. Medieval thought similarly developed conflicting approaches to the question. St. Augustine of Hippo, perhaps the most influential of all later thinkers, argued for the freedom of the will against the Manichaeans, yet supported the necessity of grace against the Pelagians. St. Thomas Aquinas concluded that "Free will becomes simply the elective power for choosing different forms of desired beatitudes." Ultimately, Scholastics, Thomists, Dominicans, Jesuits, and Molinists each developed widely diverging views of human freedom. The demonstrable variety of sources and influences is of particular interest to Milton studies, since many of the arguments adduced by earlier thinkers recur in Milton's own approach to freedom of choice in man.[3]

---

[2] John M. Steadman, *Epic and Tragic Structure in Paradise Lost* (Chicago: University of Chicago Press, 1976), p. 2; Walter Clyde Curry, *Milton's Ontology, Cosmogony, and Physics* (1957; rpt. Lexington, Kentucky: University of Kentucky Press, 1966), p. 10.

[3] Ernst F. Winter, trans. and ed., *Erasmus-Luther: Discourse on Free Will* (New York: Frederick Ungar Publishing Co., Inc., 1961), pp. 3n-4n

Of the early Fathers, Augustine was perhaps the most important participant in the dispute over the efficacy of human will and as such, a particularly strong influence on Milton. Milton's version of the Fall, for example, was essentially Augustine's, for whom disobedience was a primary factor. Yet historians and critics have noted that Augustine owed much in his intellectual outlook to pre-Christian philosophers. His dissipation as a youth, his dedication to the pageantry and rigors of Manichaeanism, and his conversion to an urbane philosophical skepticism all colored his later acceptance of Christianity. Herschel Baker refers to Augustine's intellectual and spiritual progression as a flight, a search for solace and sanctuary in a world of "political, military, and intellectual anarchy," concluding as "the most philosophical of the fathers, [who] poured the most scorn upon philosophy."[4] Augustine's thinking—influenced by Latin oratory and Neoplatonism, by paganism, Manichaeanism, and Christianity—became the foundation for the medieval view of man and of man's relation to God.

Augustine's interests and experiences prior to his conversion are important in that they explain his reactions to the theological controversies of his day. His intimate connections with the Manichaeans, for example, had instilled in him a sense of radical opposition between good and evil and a view of human nature as debased and of freedom as delusive. After his conversion, Augustine concluded that redemption and salvation were the results of divine grace freely bestowed on man by God, man neither meriting nor deserving such favor.

Augustine emphasized three basic tenets: the immense and absolute goodness of God; the total depravity of man; and the substitution of divine Will for reason as the force by which man may be perfected or elevated. The divine Will becomes the absolute good, to be neither understood nor withstood. In *Admonition and Grace*, for example, Augustine states that when God

---

[4] Baker, Herschel. *The Image of Man: A Study of the Idea of Human Dignity in Classical Antiquity, the Middle Ages, and the Renaissance* (1947; rpt. New York: Harper Torchbooks, 1961) pp. 159-160.

> wills to save a man, no human will resists Him. To say "yes" or "no" is indeed in the power of the man who says it, but in such a way that he may not thwart the will of God nor overcome His power....[5]

Augustine's insistence on the absolute Will of God in opposition to the depraved will of man led to his teachings on original sin, grace, and predestination; nor is it surprising that these tenets so closely intertwine. Augustine argues, for example, that after the fall, Adam

> was driven from paradise into exile. His whole race, corrupted by sin in him as its root, he involved in the penalty of death and condemnation: whatever offspring might be born from him and his wife (through whom he had sinned and with whom he was punished), born through carnal lust (a punishment imposed in the likeness of his disobedience), this offspring should inherent the original sin, and by this it would be drawn, through divers errors and sufferings, unto the last, endless punishment, sharing it with the fallen angels, their corrupters and masters and companions in doom. Thus "through one man sin entered into the world and through sin death, and thus death has passed into all men because all have sinned."[6]

Man's original freedom of the will was destroyed as a consequence of the fall. Man, created perfect, elected to fall. The free exercise of moral choice,

> whereby man corrupted his own self, was sufficient for his passing into sin; but to return to righteousness,

---

[5] Augustine, *Admonition and Grace,* XIV, xliii, xlv, pp. 298-299. Citations from *Admonition and Grace* are from *The Fathers of the Church* (New York: Fathers of the Church, Inc., 1947), V, 239-309.

[6] Augustine, *Enchiridion [Faith, Hope, and Charity],* VIII, xxvi, p. 392. Citations from the *Enchiridion* are from *The Fathers of the Church,* IV, 357-472.

> he has need of a Physician, since he is out of health;
> he has need of a Vivifier, because he is dead.[7]

Augustine did not totally deny freedom of choice—particularly to prelapsarian man—he did increasingly subjugate that modicum of human will to the overpowering influence of divine Will and, in his disputations with the Pelagians, was finally forced by the vigor of his arguments to deny man's ability to contribute even in the least degree to his own salvation. This extreme statement of predestination and providence strongly influenced Protestant reformers, including Luther and Calvin. In the fallen state, absolutely incapable of acting for his own restoration, no individual could even desire to be redeemed, since desire itself is predicated upon the gratuitous influence of God through grace. Man as man is nothing; his achievements come only through the outpouring of the Will of God:

> It must, therefore, be admitted that we have a will free to do both evil and good; but, in doing evil, one is free of justice and the slave of sin; on the other hand, in the matter of good no one is free unless he be freed by Him who said, "If the Son makes you free, you will be free indeed."[8]

The human will does not merit grace through the application of inherent freedom. On the contrary, it attains a degree of freedom only through grace.

Ultimately, redemption and salvation depend wholly upon the Will of God rather than upon a universal Reason which man might finally be able to understand. Citing in part Romans 8:28-30, Augustine declared that

---

[7] *On Nature and Grace*, XXV, p. 129. Citations from *Nature and Grace* are from Philip Schaff's *A Select Library of the Nicene and Post-Nicene Fathers of the Christian Church* (1887; rpt. Grand Rapids, Michigan: William B. Eerdmans Publishing Company, 1956), V.

[8] Augustine, *Admonition and Grace,* I, ii, p. 246.

> "...those whom he has predestined, them he has also called; and those whom he has called, them he has also justified, and those whom he has justified, them he has also glorified." Of their numbers no one perishes, because they are all chosen; and they are chosen because they are called according to the purpose—not their own purpose but that of God.[9]

All responsibility for man's salvation devolves finally upon God, whose Will alone lifts the onus of original sin, bestows grace, and predestines man to election or reprobation.

Although Augustinian theology generally influenced Christian dogma for thirteen centuries, however, it was not unanimously accepted, even by the contemporaries of the Bishop of Hippo. His principal opponents, Pelagius and Celestius, each accused Augustine of devising new doctrines. Julian of Eclanum represented Augustine's doctrine of original sin and grace as a personal invention and an immoral doctrine which dishonored marriage by regarding sexual concupiscence as a consequence of sin. According to Julian, Augustine favored vice by removing man's consciousness of his own strength to avoid evil.

Augustine himself recognized that his doctrines—especially predestination and the free dispensation of grace—were in a sense new. More importantly, later Church historians and theologians became aware of radical changes which entered theological speculation with Augustine, who, like Milton, was drawn simultaneously to two opposing modes of knowing: first, the rationality of non-Christian philosophies, which impelled him to beliefs not universally accepted by other Christians (particularly about the natural world) but which were essential to make Christian theology reasonable; and second, to the skepticism which denigrated man's ability to know religious truths through the exercise of reason unaided by inspiration. Thus the "classic dichotomy" between philosophical rationality and Pauline skepticism which some critics isolate as a major dilemma in Milton is as easily associated with one of the first preeminent theo-

---

[9] Augustine, *Admonition and Grace*, VII, xiv, p. 261.

logians in the Church, one whose teachings concerning predestination formed a basic doctrine of Christianity and with whose influence as a Church Father Milton would have to contend.

Augustine's great opponent in the debate over the efficacy of human will was Pelagius, whose ultra-optimism was founded on belief in the freedom of man's will and in the possibility of human perfectibility. Since Adam's fall had injured none but himself, the first man was responsible for neither human mortality nor human sinfulness. The fall was the first instance of sin, not the initial cause of it; consequently, each child is born in a state rivaling the original innocence of Adam and will sin only by imitation, not by necessity.[10]

Since most of Pelagius's writings have disappeared, what is known of his teachings is derived primarily from Augustine's responses to them. In *On the Grace of Christ*, Augustine inveighs against his opponent:

> How can this arrogant asserter of free will say, "That we are able to think a good thought comes from God but that we actually think a good thought proceeds from ourselves."

Pelagius, he further argues, had claimed that

> while we have within us a free will so strong and so stedfast [sic] against sinning, which our Maker has implanted in human nature generally, still, by His unspeakable goodness, we are further defended by His own daily help.

To which assertion Augustine replied with the question, "...what need is there of such help, if free will is so strong and so stedfast against sinning?"[11]

---

[10] J. M. Evans, *Paradise Lost and the Genesis Tradition* (Oxford: Clarendon Press, 1968), p. 92.

[11] Augustine, *On the Grace of Christ*, I, XXVI, p. 227-228. All references to this work are from Schaff's *Select Library*, V.

Augustine and Pelagius differed significantly in their evaluations of man's ability to work toward salvation. Pelagius maintained that man was created with perfect freedom to choose between good and evil and that this freedom abides in all men. Sin, to be true sin, must be committed by the free choice of the sinner; as Milton would later declare, sin compelled by necessity is not sin, neither is goodness compelled goodness. Augustine further cites Pelagius as saying:

> …we clearly and simply declare, that we possess a free will which is unimpaired for sinning and for not sinning; and this free will is in all good works *always* assisted by divine help…. In all men free will exists equally by nature, but in Christians alone is it assisted by grace.[12]

In response to the Manichaean doctrine of man's essentially evil nature, Augustine had argued that man had minimal free will and a measure of responsibility for his actions; in rebutting Pelagius, however, Augustine retreated from allowing even this modicum of choice. Never able to reconcile freedom with grace and predestination, Augustine emphasized the latter two to the virtual exclusion of the former. Pelagius, on the other hand, spurred by Augustine's disapproval and forced to strengthen his own arguments, went so far as to teach that man could achieve salvation by his own efforts. Augustine placed the responsibility on God; Pelagius removed it from God and assigned it to man.

Augustine's teachings were initially considered unorthodox. The Synod of Arles (475 A.D.) rejected Augustinian predestination, although this decree was later revoked by the Council of Orange (529 A.D.), which adopted a modified Augustinian doctrine. Among the canons of the council, four re-asserted Augustine's "personal religious philosophy":

> 7. Without grace, and merely from natural powers, we can do nothing which belongs to eternal salvation;

---

[12] Augustine, *On the Grace of Christ*, I, XXXIII, p. 229.

neither think nor will in a proper manner (*ut expedit*), nor consent to the preaching of the gospel.

13. The free will weakened in Adam is restored only by the grace of baptism.

18. Unmerited grace goes before the most meritorious works.

20. God works much good in man which man does not work; but man works good the performance of which God does not enable him to do.[13]

By 529, then, Augustine's triad of original sin, grace, and predestination had, in varying degrees, diffused throughout the Western Church. However, the disputations over moral liberty did not dissipate; not even Augustine's influence as a Church Father and an apologist could silence completely outbursts against predestination and gratuitous grace.

From the fifth century until the middle of the sixth, for example, semi-Pelagianism—or more accurately, anti-Augustinianism—developed in opposition to the harshness of Augustine's view of man. The semi-Pelagians rejected Augustinian bondage of the fallen will and claimed that

1. Whatever may be the terrible consequences of original sin, it did not entirely destroy free will. Man can have the initiative in his salvation, can alone produce salutary acts, can begin to believe. Justification once merited…he can by his personal efforts persevere in the right way of justification; he would consequently have the first word and the last in the matter of his salvation.

---

[13] Charles Joseph Hefele, *A History of the Councils of the Church from the Original Documents* (1895; rpt. AMS reprint, 1972), IV, 152-169. See also Evans, pp. 110-111.

2. All men are equally called to salvation and receive sufficient grace in order to realize it. It all depends upon the will of man and each one merits his election or reprobation.

3. There is then no absolute predestination; it is horrible blasphemy to say that God cannot save all men and that the predestination of the elect and the reprobation of the damned are anterior to the foresight of the merits of the ones and the demerits of the others.[14]

Among the semi-Pelagians clustered in Gaul, the poets Hilary, Victor, Avitus, and Cyprian treated, among other things, the narrative of the Fall of Man. Though influenced only marginally by Pelagius, they wrote in opposition to Augustine, denying his teaching that man was incapable of good, since such a belief would contravene any value in the monastic system of which the poets were part. For the semi-Pelagians, man could be at least proximately responsible for stimulating salvation.[15]

Augustine's views on man, sin, grace, and predestination, while providing in a highly modified form the basis for centuries of Catholic doctrine, were never accepted in their full severity by the Church as a whole; Cassian, Gregory the Great, Isidore of Seville, and Aldhelm were among the many who viewed man more optimistically than strict Augustinianism might allow.[16] At best, the dogma of the Church allowed only for compromise between the extremes of Pelagian free will and Augustinian predestination; and both extremes continued as viable alternative explanations of human actions until Milton's time and beyond.

---

[14] James Barker, *Apostasy from the Divine Church* (private publication: Kate Montgomery Barker, 1960), p. 487. See also Orvil Glade Hunsaker's "Calvinistic Election and Arminian Reparation," Diss. The University of Illinois at Urbana-Champaign, 1970, p. 54.

[15] Evans, pp. 110-112.

[16] Evans, p. 166.

* * * * * * *

From the ninth century until the beginnings of the Italian Renaissance in the fifteenth, the debate over the freedom of the human will continued. Among others, Boethius had reacted strongly to the belief in the bondage of man's will. In fact, Boethian emphasis on the freedom of the will served as a springboard for one of the initial Renaissance contributions to the discussion of human will, Lorenzo Valla's *Dialogue on Free Will*. Valla refuted the conclusions of the fifth book of Boethius's *Consolatio* by remarking:

> Listen, for this is what I wished to say: Paul first said, "so then it is not of him that willeth, nor of [man] that runneth, but of God that showeth mercy." But Boethius in his whole argument concludes, not actually in words but in substance; "It is not of God who foreseeth, but of man who willeth and runneth."[17]

In the *Dialogue*, Valla attacks Aristotelian and Scholastic attempts at reconciling freedom and divine providence, not by adhering strictly to predestination and grace as Augustine had done, but by denying the capability of the human intellect to conceive of any solution to the paradox. Valla "consistently and comprehensively emphasized the irreconcilability of reason and faith, of philosophy and theology, of paganism and Christianity,"[18] declaring as Augustine had before him that philosophy was the enemy of theology and that earlier heresies had derived almost entirely from philosophic sources, much to the detriment and rarely to the aid of the Church.

The thesis of the *Dialogue* is in fact two-fold: "Whether the foreknowledge of God stands in the way of free will and whether

---

[17] Valla, Lorenzo, *Dialogue on Free Will*, trans. Charles Edward Trinkaus, in *The Renaissance Philosophy of Man*, ed. Ernst Cassirer, Paul Oskar Kristeller, and John Herman Randall, Jr., (1948; rpt. Chicago: The University of Chicago Press, 1971), p. 179.

[18] Valla, p. 149.

Boethius has correctly argued this question."[19] After proving to his own satisfaction that Boethius was incorrect, Valla tackles the question of freedom itself. He defines the relationship between foreknowledge and freedom by using Jupiter and Apollo to represent two manifestations of God—will and foreknowledge. Apollo's foreknowledge does not necessitate evil on the part of man; hence man is not necessitated to action by the omniscience of God. Jupiter's will, on the other hand, being a metaphor for the undeviatingly wise and good will of God, determines man's actions. Thus

> although the wisdom of God cannot be separated from His power and will, I may by this device of Apollo and Jupiter separate them. What cannot be achieved with one god may be achieved with two, each having his proper nature—the one for creating the character of men, the other for knowing—that it may appear that providence is not the cause of necessity but that all this whatever it is must be referred to the will of God.[20]

Valla insists, however, that retreating to the will of God as final arbitrator of man's actions does not eliminate free will:

> Now, indeed, He brings no necessity, and His hardening one and showing another mercy does not deprive us of free will since He does this most wisely and in full holiness.[21]

This solution—that freedom is granted to some through the unlimited goodness and will of God—is close to Luther's doctrine of the gift of grace extended to the elect. Faith in the goodness of God provides a partial reconciliation between will and foreknowledge, while the final answer is simply not to ask the question:

---

[19] Valla, p. 161.
[20] Valla, p. 174.
[21] Valla, p. 177.

> Let us therefore shun greedy knowledge of high things, condescending rather to those of low estate. For nothing is of greater avail for Christian men than to feel humble. In this way we are more aware of the magnificence of God, whence it is written (I Peter 5:5); "God resisteth the proud and giveth grace to the humble." To attain this grace I will no longer be anxious about this question lest by investigating the majesty of God I be blinded by His light.[22]

In his insistence on the divine over the human, Valla bridges the viewpoints in the dispute over human will; he looks back to patristics, yet shares the classicism and learning of the Italian humanism of Marsilio Ficino and Giovanni Pico della Mirandola. Valla was always insistent, however, that learning must be controlled. His writings became for Erasmus a proof of the difficulty of arguing against the freedom of the will, since,

> From Apostolic times to this day there was no writer hitherto who totally denied the force of free will, save Manichaeus and John Wycliffe alone. For Lorenzo Valla, who almost seems to agree with them, has little authority among theologians of weight.[23]

Luther and Calvin, on the other hand, welcomed Valla as a proponent of grace, although Calvin notes that Valla had shown "that this controversy is unnecessary because both life and death are acts of God's will rather than of his foreknowledge."[24] Like Milton, Valla was confronted by classical and Christian arguments for and against

---

[22] Valla, p. 181.

[23] Desiderius Erasmus, *On Free Will*, trans. Ernst F. Winter, in *Erasmus-Luther*, pp. 14-15. See also Trinkaus's introduction to Valla in Ernst Cassirer and others, eds., *The Renaissance Philosophy of Man* (1948; rpt. Chicago: University of Chicago Press, 1971), p. 153.

[24] Ernst Cassirer and others, *The Renaissance Philosophy of Man*, p. 152.

man's moral freedom; unlike Milton, however, he concluded that freedom emanates from God alone, not from man.

Although Valla ultimately retreated to faith and avoidance of final questioning of man's moral freedom, others of his nation and time were not so hesitantly conservative. The optimism which was one of the legacies of the Renaissance and which derived from a synthesis of medieval rationalistic theology and the humanistic tradition of classical antiquity is perhaps nowhere so clearly evident as in the writings of Ficino and Pico. Fully aware of the double truths of classical philosophy and Christianity's incremental doctrines, and equally aware of the breakdown of the Augustinian dualism between spirit and matter, Ficino and Pico arrived at a near apotheosis of man.

Ficino's goal was to harmonize Platonic philosophy and historical Christianity; his universe of concentric circles emanating from God merged Christianity with the Neoplatonic commonplace of an essentially good universe. In Ficino's hierarchy, man's soul is the third of five essences, the "fountain of motion." Because of his central position, man—and man only—has affinities with forms above and below himself in the hierarchy and may ascend or descend according to his choices. Although the intellect (striving for knowledge of all things) and the will (striving for enjoyment of all things) fundamentally frustrate each other, they both attain fulfillment through possession of the infinite source of all knowledge and enjoyment, that is, God.[25]

Ficino denies, however, that man can achieve the final End, the Good, without assistance from external grace. Possession of reason, which alone differentiates man from the brutes below and the angels above, continually frustrates man:

> Nothing indeed can be imagined more unreasonable
> than that man, who through reason is the most perfect
> of all animals, nay of all things under heaven, most

---

[25] *The Image of Man*, pp. 244-245. See also Josephine Burroughs' introduction to Ficino in Cassirer and others, eds., *The Renaissance Philosophy of Man*, pp. 190-192.

> perfect, I say, with regard to that formal perfection which is bestowed upon us from the beginning, that man, also through reason should be the least perfect of all with regard to that final perfection for the sake of which the first perfection is given. This seems to be that most unfortunate Prometheus. Instructed by the divine wisdom of Pallas, he gained possession of the heavenly fire, that is, reason. Because of this very possession, on the very highest peak of the mountain, that is, at the very height of contemplation, he is rightly judged most miserable of all, for he is made wretched by the continual gnawing of the most venous of vultures, that is, by the torments of inquiry.[26]

Man is endowed with reason which frustrates the will. That frustration necessitates further aid in order for man to reach the Good; and that aid is

> none other than infinite power itself. This power, conformably with the free nature of the will, moves in the mind in a certain manner which is in the highest degree free toward the paths to be chosen; while conformably with the infinite power of the moving cause, it urges the mind toward the desired end, so much so that the mind cannot fail to strive after that end.[27]

Since man is above the brutes by virtue of his reason and powers of contemplation, and potentially above the angels themselves by virtue of divine worship, he is able to draw nearer to God and ultimately to participate—as Milton would later also suggest—in knowledge of God, the "fountain of blessedness." Indeed, precisely because of these elements in his make-up, man may "at some time

---

[26] Marcilio Ficino, "Five Questions Concerning the Mind," in Ernst Cassirer, and others, eds., *The Renaissance Philosophy of Man*, p. 208.
[27] Ficino, "Five Questions," pp. 210-211.

be much more blessed than they in the possession of his desired end":

> This is necessary in order that he who is more similar to the celestial beings, both because of the ardor of the will and because of the light of intelligence, may be, in like manner, more similar to them in happiness of life, for the power and excellence of thinking and willing originate from the power of life.[28]

Possessing capacities beyond those of the brutes below and the angels above, man is the cherished creation of God in an anthropocentric universe. He is the superlative, the "chain of the world, the face of all, and the knot and bond of the universe."[29]

Pico, Ficino's pupil, was even more enthusiastic than his teacher about human freedom. For Pico, all other levels of creation are bounded by their inherent natures; only man resides in the center of creation and enjoys the power to rise toward God or fall to the state of beasts. Having created man expressly to appreciate the vastness of creation, God placed him in the middle of that creation and instructed him that

> whatever place, whatever form, whatever gifts you may, with premeditation, select, these same you may have and possess through your own judgment and decision. The nature of all other creatures is defined and restricted within laws which We have laid down; you, by contrast, impeded by no such restrictions, may, by your own free will, to whose custody We have assigned you, trace for yourselves the lineaments of your own nature.[30]

---

[28] Ficino, "Five Questions," p. 211.
[29] Baker, *The Image of Man*, p. 244.
[30] Giovanni Pico della Mirandola, *Oration on the Dignity of Man*, trans. A. Robert Caponigri (Chicago: Henry Regnery Company, 1956), p. 7. See also Battista Gelli's popularized treatment of the same point in Robert Adams's *The Circe*

Pico goes beyond Ficino in defining man's ability to progress or regress through conscious moral choice. For Ficino, reason and will alone could not impel man to his final end; for Pico, man is the initiator of action. His high function is to raise himself. The brutes are, "from the moment of their birth," all that they can ever be; the "highest spiritual beings" were fixed in the "mode of being which would be theirs through measureless eternities" soon after their creation; but man is endowed with the "seeds pregnant with all possibilities, the germs of every form of life." Man may choose which potential to fulfill:

> If vegetative, he will become a plant; if sensual, he will become brutish; if intellectual, he will be an angel and the son of God. And if, dissatisfied with the lot of all creatures, he should recollect himself to the center of his own unity, he will there become one spirit with God, in the solitary darkness of the Father, Who is set above all things....[31]

Man thus dwells on the margins of two worlds and, "supernatural and contingent on nothing save himself," determines which world he will inherit. He is released even from the need for grace to initiate repentance and regeneration.[32]

By pressing Ficino's original arguments to an almost Pelagian conclusion, Pico introduces a theme which will recur throughout the Renaissance, culminating in Milton's *Areopagitica*: man has reason—choice—and by his reason he may learn to know God. As Baker summarizes Pico's philosophy, "Man may wallow in the mud, but he reaches to the stars."[33] Ficino's religious philosophy and

---

of Signior Giovanni Battista Gelli (Ithaca, New York: Cornell University Press, 1963) p. 175.

[31] Pico, *Oration*, pp. 8-9.

[32] Baker, *The Image of Man*, p. 245.

[33] Baker, *The Image of Man*, p. 217. See also Edward S. LeComte, "*Areopagitica* as a Scenario for *Paradise Lost*," in *Achievements of the Left Hand*, ed.

Pico's apotheosis of human choice represent the final refinements of one approach to the question of freedom, an approach echoed in such diverse writers as Gelli, Vives, Linacre, Colet, Erasmus, More, Eliot, Sidney, Spenser, and finally Milton.

* * * * * * *

By the beginning of the Reformation, then, the dispute over humanity's moral freedom had bifurcated. Theology and philosophy both carried weight as modes of perceiving truth. Proponents and opponents of the freedom of the human will could both argue by appealing to authorities who had already clearly defined the terms and positions of the debate. In general, those who accepted human freedom of choice drew their arguments at least in part from the Neoplatonism of the Florentine Academy, from various "heretical" writings of the early Fathers (Origen, Pelagius, and others), or from the radically modified Augustinianism of the Middle Ages. Opponents of the human will, on the other hand, countered with strict Augustinian predestination, careful interpretation of the Scriptures, and rejection of philosophical speculation. This division is central to the debates between Erasmus and Luther, an almost archetypal confrontation between belief in human freedom and belief in the bondage of the human will.

When Erasmus finally agreed to combat Luther and the violent reforms which the latter was advocating, he chose to do so on a point at which he clearly differed from Luther, the problem of "good and evil, guilt and compulsion, liberty and bondage, God and man." He drew upon a variety of traditions, arguing that the Scriptures, the Church Fathers and doctors, philosophers both classical and Christian, and human reason all affirmed freedom of choice, "the power

---

Michael Lieb and John T. Shawcross (Amherst, Massachusetts: The University of Massachusetts Press, 1974), pp. 121-141.

of the human will whereby man can apply to or turn away from that which leads unto eternal salvation."[34]

Fearful of the endeavors of reformers to replace medieval rational theology with Augustinian revelation, Erasmus argued that belief in man's moral freedom had been widespread in the historical Church. He included Origen, Basil, Chrysostom, Cyril, John Damascene, Theophylactus, Tertullian, Cyprian, Hilary, Jerome, Augustine, Aquinas, Duns Scotus, Durandus of Saint-Pourçain, John Capreolus, Gabriel Biel, Giles of Rome, Gregory of Rimini, and Alexander of Hales in his list of proponents of free will. He noted that early non-Christians had observed the world and gained a knowledge of divine goodness and kindness without the aid of Scriptures or revelation; they had in fact wills tending toward moral good but incapable of eternal salvation without the additional impetus of grace through faith.[35] He cited both the Old and the New Testaments to support free will, mentioning in addition references to admonition and repentance which presupposed the ability of man to make moral choices. Such scriptures would be meaningless if there were no actual human capacity to discriminate between alternatives.

Erasmus carefully avoided involving himself in the extremes of the dispute. He rejected the heresy of Pelagius:

> Pelagius taught that no new grace was needed once grace had liberated and healed the free will of man. Thus the free will by itself was deemed sufficient to achieve eternal salvation. But we owe salvation solely to God without whose grace the will of man could not be effectively free to achieve good.[36]

---

[34] Winter, p. 20. Note also Johann Huizinga, *Erasmus and the Age of Reformation* (New York: Harper Torchbooks, 1957), pp. 161-169; Baker, *The Image of Man*, pp. 266-274, 313-333.
[35] Winter, pp. 13-14, 24.
[36] Winter, p. 26.

But he was also chary of strict Augustinian predestination, the hopelessness of final condemnation which he identified with Luther. He concluded that

> although the free will has been wounded through sin, it is not extinct; though it has contracted a paralysis, making us before the reception of grace more readily inclined towards evil than good, free will has not been destroyed. Only to the extent that monstrous crimes or the habit of sin, having become our second nature, dim at times the judgment of the intellect and bury thereby the free will does the former seem destroyed and the latter dead.[37]

For Erasmus, the vast preponderance of data—theological, philosophical, historical, and rational—witnesses the inherent liberty of man to determine by his choices his ultimate state. And in Erasmus, according to Ruth Bartholomew, Milton found his first satisfactorily "reasoned exposition of the doctrine of free will."[38]

On the other side of the debate, Luther (and later Calvin) demanded a denial of rational theology. Luther found the belief that man could presume to know God, that God must thereby be circumscribed by the boundaries of reason, abhorrent. Luther's alternative was a return to a dogmatic Augustinianism, from which he claimed the main tenets of Reformation doctrine—justification by faith, original sin, and predestination—were drawn. Luther's part in the debate was thus primarily theological, buttressed by scriptures, as opposed to Erasmus's essentially humanistic approach.

Erasmus had clearly established the dimensions of the gulf separating himself from Luther when, in the *De Libero Arbitrio*, he had cited Luther's own *Assertio*:

---

[37] Winter, p. 26.
[38] Ruth Bartholomew, "Some Sources of Milton's Doctrine of Free Will," Diss. Western Reserve University, 1945, iv-v.

> I have expressed it improperly when I said that the free will, before obtaining grace, is really an empty name. I should have said straightforwardly that the free will is really a fiction, and a label without reality, because it is in no man's power to plan any evil or good. As the article of Wycliffe, condemned at Constance, correctly teaches; everything takes place by absolute necessity.

For Luther,

> It is then essentially necessary and wholesome for Christians to know that God foreknows nothing contingently, but that he foresees, purposes and does all things according to his immutable, eternal, and infallible will. This thunderbolt throws free will flat and utterly dashes it to pieces. Those who want to assert it must either deny this thunderbolt or pretend not to see it....[39]

Luther could find nothing in the Church Fathers or in revealed Scripture to support Erasmus's contention that the human will is free.

Calvin—like Luther before him—was among the most influential of the reformers, yet his views on predestination and the bondage of the will were similarly countered and modified by an advocate of the freedom of the will, Arminius. Initially, the division between Calvinism and Arminianism stemmed from a fundamental disagreement over the efficacy of the Atonement. Calvin held that the elect alone were affected by an infallible Atonement, while Arminius taught a universal Atonement, contingent upon the exercise of faith. Arminius further rejected Calvin's claims that, since God created the world—including, of course, man—out of nothing, all things good or evil depend ultimately upon the will of the Creator.

---

[39] Winter, p. 106.

Calvinism was based upon five strict principles: (1) since the gift of faith extends only to those under eternal decree of election (predestination), the elect cannot be cast off or their numbers diminished; (2) the mercy of the Atonement extends only to the elect; (3) man suffers the consequences of original sin; (4) man's self-regeneration is impossible; and (5) God, having granted grace, confirms it always. Against these five tenets, Arminianism proposed its own five: (1) the decree of salvation refers to those who believe and persevere in the faith; (2) the Atonement is sufficient for all men, but only the faithful will benefit; (3) man can reject the call of God and refuse grace and faith; (4) man can fail to persevere to the end; and (5) even though man inherits original sin and depravity, he has freedom of the will to overcome that depravity and to accept or reject the gift of salvation.[40] Arminianism thus adumbrates (and perhaps in part accounts for) Milton's later modification of the absolutism of Calvinistic decree with conditional decrees, through which the supremacy of the divine will allows man some choice in overcoming or submitting to depravity.

Arminius distinguished among five freedoms relating to the will: freedom from control by one who commands, from government by a superior, from necessity, from sin, and from misery. The first two apply exclusively to God, the fifth to prelapsarian man, and the third and fourth to fallen man. Freedom from necessity is essential to the will, but Arminius (unlike Pelagius) denied that an unnecessitated will is therefore free from sin. Sinful man is free, but not to perform meritorious acts.[41] Arminius cites Bernard of Clairvaux to the effect that

> Take away free will and nothing will be left to be saved. Take away grace, and nothing will be left as the source of salvation. This work cannot be effected

---

[40] Milton J. Backman, Jr., *American Religions and the Rise of* Mormonism (Salt Lake City: Deseret Book Company, 1970), pp. 86-87; Joseph Moody McDill, *Milton and the Pattern of Calvinism* (Folcroft, Pennsylvania: The Folcroft Press, 1969) pp. 38-40.

[41] Bangs, pp. 340-341.

> without two parties—one, from whom it may come; the other, to whom or in whom it may be wrought. God is the author of salvation. Free will only is capable of being saved.

Although man is not self-sufficient, he does participate in restoration through cooperating in believing. Man

> loves and embraces that which is good, just, and holy, and…being made capable in Christ, cooperating now with God, he prosecutes the good which he knows and loves, and he begins to perform it in deed.[42]

Grace is sufficient to the "beginning, continuation, and consummation of faith"; yet that grace is not the irresistible force of Augustine, but rather a personal influence, the love "with which God loves men absolutely to salvation...and according to which he absolutely intends to bestow upon them eternal life."[43]

Arminian teachings infiltrated many Protestant groups, including those which developed in England during Milton's youth. Indeed, until the Westminster Confession of 1647, English Calvinism was itself marked by a strong strain of Arminianism, a particularly interesting phenomenon in view of Milton's close affinities at different times with both schools of doctrine.

In sixteenth- and seventeenth-century England, the dispute over man's moral liberty or bondage made itself felt in various—and occasionally surprising—ways. As early as the reign of Elizabeth, the English had in part incorporated arguments for the freedom of the will into their national identification of England with the new Chosen People, a theme which extended well into Milton's lifetime. Conversely, the proponents of the bondage of the will began to apply the theological arguments of Luther and Calvin to their daily lives.

---

[42] Bangs, p. 341.
[43] Bangs, pp. 350-351.

As early as the publication of Foxe's *Book of Martyrs* and the accession of Elizabeth, English apologists attempted to relate the histories of the Marian martyrs to the larger destiny of the English, the new Chosen People. Aided by a popular (and carefully cultivated) association of Elizabeth with rejuvenated Arthurian traditions and with the image of Astraea, Goddess of Justice and harbinger of the new Golden Age, the English expanded their identification as Chosen People throughout the reigns of Elizabeth, James I, and Charles I. With the inception of the Commonwealth and the rule of the Saints, the ideal seemed at fruition. Popular preachers referred to the greatness of England's destiny and urged Parliament to fulfill the covenant which God had made with England and which had been disturbed by the Laudian episcopacy, but emphasized that the realization of that promise was contingent upon the choices and decisions made by the English people.

The individual elements of the ideal—Elizabeth, Astraea, England's destiny, and apocalyptic history—combined to elevate the importance of human dignity and freedom. If the New Jerusalem were to be established, each individual must live up to the necessary covenants; if the Golden Age were to return, each individual must be free to prepare for it. When public figures such as Bishop Jewel, Bishop Aylmer, Lancelot Andrewes, and Peter Marshall spoke of the destiny of England, of the coming of the Golden Age and the New Jerusalem, and of the responsibility of fulfilling a covenant with God, they presupposed man's freedom to choose and act. Similarly, Milton's writings often assume the possibility of individual reformation, so that "Time will run back and fetch the Age of Gold."

In addition to theological and political effects, predestinarian teachings (and their reverse, advocacy of human freedom) also had definite popular influences in England. In the *De Libero Arbitrio*, Erasmus had argued that even if the case against the freedom of the will were valid, it would be worse than pointless to publish it, since man would then be absolved of all moral responsibility for sin. Man is "lazy, indolent, malicious, and in addition, incorrigibly prone to every impious outrage"; why make it even worse by telling him that he is not the ultimate source of the evil he does and that he has no choice in the matter?[44]

At least one segment of the seventeenth-century population took the dispute between predestination and the free will so seriously that, in total disregard of Erasmus's warnings, they despaired of salvation and in its place embraced licentious pleasure. Predestinarian theologians had warned that none should assume damnation, but

> not everyone had a Calvin's assurance, and if, as Augustine had said, the elect constitute a crew (*societas*) in which the damned had no part, perhaps those who feared that they were damned may have needed their own anti-society to confront the separated congregations of the Reformation.[45]

During the first half of the century, a group popularly known as "The Devil's Crew" (usually associated with Sir Edmund Baynham, an exiled participant in the Gunpowder Plot) apparently accepted their probable damnation as fact and lived accordingly. Baynham's following, a group who "were thought to be reprobate with the devils in Hell—'of the damned crew,' King James called them—probably thought as much themselves and challenged the worst." The frequent stigmatization of the "Damned Crew" as following "out of this doctrine of predestination which the priuate spirit inuented, *Caluin* diuulged, *Machiauell* confirmed, and the Diuell by all liberty of sinne, and rebellion hath increased and propagated"[46] suggests the intensity to which the dispute between free will and predestination attained during Milton's time.

The most obvious influence of Baynham and his crew on Milton, according to S. E. Sprott, appears in the Nativity Ode. The ode, with its "Damned Crew," contains what seems to be a direct reference to Baynham (l. 228). Sprott neglects to point out, however, that throughout the major poetry Milton most frequently employs the

---

[44] Winter, p. 11.
[45] S. E. Sprott, "The Damned Crew," *PMLA*, LXXXIV, 3 (May 1969), p. 498.
[46] Sprott, p. 499

word "crew" in just the negative sense that Sprott attempts to define. Only in "L'Allegro" (37-40) is the word used to suggest a loosely unified band or company. In the remainder of the poetry "crew" is generally condemnatory and either directly or indirectly relevant to demons and devils.

These, then, are among the more important of the varied traditions which Milton had at his disposal when solving for himself the thorny problem of man's moral freedom. Like others of his time, he could draw from pre-Christian philosophy, Christian dogma, medieval synthesis, humanism, and Reformation Protestantism. The way in which he responded to these influences relates directly to Milton's position in the centuries-old dispute.

Milton was passionately dedicated to freedom in literary, theological, political, and individual contexts. One approach to assessing Milton's use of the traditions surrounding freedom of choice in his writings is to examine them in practice in Milton's life as he perceived it. Autobiographical passages relating to conscious choices occur frequently and, at times, in some rather unusual public venues. The earliest, his comments on deliberative alternatives in "At a Vacation Exercise in the College," concerns his choice of vehicle for his native language, "some graver subject" (29), duly and splendidly dressed in the "richest Robes" English has to offer. In his only adult piece written in heroic couplets, he introduces the topic with a quasi-epic invocation to his "native Language," then proceeds to speak directly to his college audience of his strengths, weaknesses, and aspirations as a poet. He follows this moment of illumination on his sense of vocation by listing further possible options open to him as poet: exalted lyrics, poems of gods and creation, or epics on great "Kings and Queens and *Heroes* old" (47). Then, as if suddenly noticing his unwonted foray into autobiography, he recalls himself to the present occasion and introduces the next scene in the college entertainment. Coming as it does after his two childhood psalm exercises, a translation of Horace, and a sequence of increasingly complex and ambitious poems in Latin, his decision to speak in English verse about English verse before a public audience suggests how important the moment was for him. There is admittedly little sense here of a deep philosophical debate on moral agency or free will, but the lines to suggest how important thoughtful, considered choice was to the burgeoning poet.

Similarly, "Elegy VI," written for his childhood friend Charles Diodati, in part concerns a choice between lyric and epic, while at the same time indicating Milton's arrogation of absolute freedom in how the true poet much choose to live his life. This assumption of purity and austerity, raising the poet to the elevation of Poet-Priest, whether intended seriously or playfully, is important as it relates to the poet's conscious choices of vocation and poetic form.

Over a decade later, when Milton published his first prose tracts, he again takes the opportunity to infuse public statements with his own private beliefs. "The Preface" to *The Reason of Church Government*, written in first person, indicates that Milton's primary criterion for true law is based on choice. Citing both Plato and Moses as exemplars, he immediately asserts that the purpose of his tract is not to force subjection to his opinions but rather to demonstrate truth through reasoned argument that would in turn incite agreement through "choice and purpose." Only later, in the introduction to the Second Book does he abruptly digress from a reasoned explication of church government to an extended autobiographical sketch, beginning with disparaging his ability to write in prose and declaring his credentials as a poet (although his name would have been nearly unknown among his contemporaries at this point) and leading into his debate on whether to commit himself to writing the several varieties and topics of lyric, tragedy, or epic poetry. Only then does he return to his stated topic.

In subsequent tracts, with his increasing notoriety as spokesman for the Commonwealth, he will find further opportunities (discussed below) to resort to autobiography to give warrant to his writings, his life, and his choices

In addition to this circumstantial evidence of autobiographical alternative, it is of note that Milton was aware of and drew from each of the various backgrounds discussed in this chapter. He shows affinities with classical thinkers, Christian dogmatists and apologists, Reformation propagandists, and contemporary writers; yet ultimately, Milton is never exclusively indebted to any of these. He created his own definition of liberty and endowed his poetic universe with that liberty. Milton remained relatively untouched, for example, by the arguments adduced by Augustine to deny the freedom of the will. And, even though Milton was aware of Christian arguments for free will, he relied largely on his own proofs, many of which tended to be more pre-Christian than Christian. With Aristotle, for example, Milton held men responsible only for those transgressions committed in the presence of viable alternatives. Milton did not, of course, cut himself off completely from the traditions of Christian exegesis; like others of his time, he cites both the later Fathers and the writings of the primitive Church prior to the encroachment of Hellenistic philosophy and Eastern mysteries.

Several critics—including C. M. Bowra and George Conklin—have argued that although Milton embraced elements of Neoplatonism and humanism, he also drew heavily from Calvinism.[47] William B. Hunter, Jr., on the other hand, suggests that the format of the 1645 edition of the poems resembled an Arminian spiritual autobiography, characteristics of which also appeared in Izaak Walton's *Lives*, Edward Herbert's *Autobiography*, and Sir Thomas Browne's *Religio Medici*.[48] Yet finally, it is impossible to equate Milton simply with the Calvinists or with the Arminians. His eclecticism allowed him to draw from each and still remain uniquely Milton.

At roughly the same time that Milton's early leanings toward Calvinism were being modified by his exposure to Arminianism, he also began to share in England's millenary hopes. When the once-distant visions of the English reformers suddenly seemed within reach, Milton entered the struggle, urging his fellow-Englishmen to regeneration and reform, reasserting as the new Chosen People, the "strong and puissant nation" of *Areopagitica,* the legends of English past, national destiny, and the return of the Astraean Golden Age. He hailed Parliament with the same apocalyptic fervor as had Foxe, Jewel, Aylmer, and others in writing of Elizabeth. This optimism largely informs the early prose and poetry, and perhaps accounts for

---

[47] C. M. Bowra, . *From Virgil to Milton.* 1945; rpt. London: Macmillan, 1967.p. 216; George Newton Conklin, *Biblical Criticism and Heresy in Milton.* (Columbia University, New York: King's Crown Press, 1949), p. 9;

[48] Hunter, "John Milton: Autobiographer," pp. 100-101.

his appropriation of the phrase "Damned Crew" in several poems. Later, Milton replaced his belief in a national destiny with a retreat into the world of private reformation and freedom, the "Paradise within" of the final poems. Regardless of his use of specific sources, however, Milton constantly defended his passionate advocacy of the ideals of liberty and of the freedom of man to direct his own course.

CHAPTER TWO

Toward a Definition of Liberty—
The Early Poetry and the Prose

> The light which we have gained, was given us, not to be ever staring on, but by it to discover onward things more remote from our knowledge. It is not the unfrocking of a priest, the unmitering of a bishop, and the removing him from off the Presbyterian shoulders that will make us a happy nation; no, if other things as great in the church, and in the rule of life both economical and political, be not looked into and reformed, we have looked so long upon the blaze that Zwinglius and Calvin hath beaconed up to us, that we are stark blind.—*Areopagitica*

i. The Early Minor Poems

Milton's interest in the complexities of liberty and freedom of choice arises early in his career. Among Milton's first poems is a paraphrase of Psalm 114, "done by the author at fifteen years old" which begins:

> When the blest seed of *Terah's* faithful Son,
> After long toil their liberty had won,
> And past from *Pharian* fields to *Canaan* Land,
> Led by the strength of the Almighty's hand,

> *Jehovah's* wonders were in *Israel* shown,
> His praise and glory was in *Israel* known.
>
> (1-6)

These lines contain much that is embryonically Miltonic: rhythmical repetition of phrases, circumlocutory renaming of characters and events to suggest more appropriate, more richly meaningful allusions, and exploitation of elevated poetic diction. More specifically, however, they also foreshadow Milton's abiding concern with liberty and responsibility. When compared to the original version as translated in the King James Bible,

> When Israel went out of Egypt, the house of Jacob from a people of strange language;
>
> Judah was his sanctuary, *and* Israel his dominion,
>
> (114: 1-2)

Milton's paraphrase not only suggests the labor on the part of the Seed of Abraham—their "long toil" as slaves in Egypt—but also adumbrates their "long toil" of forty years and more to confirm their liberty. Milton's use of the verb *won* identifies the "blest seed" as conscious actors, at least partially responsible for their restoration to full external liberty, since all references in the *Oxford English Dictionary* to the verb *win* which might have been available to Milton connote volition and active striving. The word seems not to have been used passively, that is, in a sense which would have allowed the newly acquired freedom of the Israelites to have been granted to them by an external grace rather than achieved by them through some individual effort. Even the poetic re-naming of Abraham as "*Terah's* faithful son" emphasizes Abraham's decision to abandon the idolatry of his father for the worship of the true God. The scriptural account, on the other hand, does not mention overtly any such workings of will on the part of Terah's sons; the actor becomes the neutral and collective *Israel,* the verb *went* carries no strong implications of striving, and the tenor of the passage does indeed represent the Israel's freedom as an external manifestation of God's grace to His chosen people.

It is consistent with Milton's later views and methods that even this early he should expand the bare-bones scriptural reference and in doing so intrude an element of human will. Milton's characters continually confront temptations or choices; they are typically defiant or defensive in the face of opposition. Truth and virtue may—in fact, *must*—triumph, but only after testing and trial. In the psalm, the short phrase "After long toil their liberty had won" expresses this sense of trial and testing. And just as the Israelites, after four centuries of servitude, reassert their national identity as Chosen People by obedience and righteous choice, so all humans enjoy the freedom to choose and win for themselves true liberty—if not absolute political liberty, then at the very least that internal liberty on which all external liberty depends.

The companion paraphrase, Psalm 136, similarly uses grammatical and linguistic structures to underpin the centrality of volition in obedience. The King James Version couches the opening verses in the imperative—"O give thanks unto the LORD…. O give thanks unto the God of Gods." Action moves from an external source to Israel, commanding them to offer up thanks. Milton's paraphrase inverts that direction and provides an intimacy of actor that the original lacks: "Let us…." The decision to praise is *ours* in response to God's actions, including delivering us from "wrathful tyrants," who by Milton's definition in the *Tenure of Kings and Magistrates* exemplified imposed will (and who do not appear in the original), and freeing "us from our slavery." Again, the King James Version is far more neutral, shifting emphasis from Israel's slavery to God's redemptive act (136: 24).

In the brief "Apologus de Rustico et Hero" (c. 1625), Milton provides a glimpse at the consequence of impercipient choice. Desiring a larger share of succulent fruit, a landlord transplants an ancient tree (that it is an apple tree seems more than coincidence) from the country to his city garden. There it suffers from transplant shock and dies, leaving the landlord to mourn his greediness and the loss of even a relatively small harvest. Although perhaps not a major feature in the verse-exercise, the sense of Milton's concern for proper choice and the consequences of improper choice filters through.

The subsequent Latin epistle to Charles Diodati, "Elegy I" (1626), deals with Milton's activities while rusticated from Cambridge for a term. Among other things, Milton bewails the cause of his suspension, his being "constantly subjected to the threats of a rough tutor and to other indignities which my spirit cannot endure." His preference for freedom in "exile" in London to curtailed liberty at Cambridge allows him opportunity to explore activities more congenial to his sense of vocation: to dedicate himself to the Muses, to attend the theater, to describe in high heroic style the beauties of the maidens he watches from a distance. Only in the final lines does the impetus for action shift from the young narrator to those who control his life: "It is decided that I am to go back to the reedy fens of the Cam and return again to the hum of the noisy school."[49] A stridently active and volitive letter concludes in a brief acknowledgement of forced passivity.

While none of these poems seem intended to bear the weight of intense theological reasoning on the subject of free will and moral agency, there appears in them at least a rudimentary concern with liberty and choice. In a subsequent work, however, this rudimentary concern becomes more overt as Milton (later a defender of the regicides) composed *In Quintum Novembris* (1626), in which he celebrates the monarchy of the "establisher of peace," the "devout James" as a manifestation of England's destiny, and contrasts the concord of James' reign with the machinations and discord of Devils and Popes. Order opposes disorder; English freedom under James opposes the bondage of Machiavellian, demonic slavery:

> The establisher of peace was seated on his new throne, fortunate and affluent, with no suspicion of a secret conspiracy or of a foe, when the cruel tyrant who governs the fiery streams of Acheron, the father of the Eumenides, the wandering outcast from the ce-

---

[49] Merritt Y. Hughes, *John Milton: Complete Poems and Major Prose* (New York: Odyssey Press, 1957), p. 10.

> lestial Olympus, chanced to range through the vast circle of the earth, counting the companions of his wickedness, his faithful slaves, who are destined after their miserable deaths to take their share in his kingdom. (Hughes, 15)

The "cruel tyrant" unleashes his anger against England, the land of peace and plenty, but even more against the sight of free obedience: "...and—what irked him worse—a people worshipping the sacred deity of the true God...." (Hughes, 16)

For the young Milton, English Protestantism under James promised the fulfillment of the millenarian hopes which had developed throughout the reign of Elizabeth. The demon of *In Quintum Novembris*, the "dark lord of shadows, the ruler of the speechless dead," sees the religion of Jacobean England as the sole threat to his sovereignty over the earth: "After wandering throughout the whole world," says he, "I find this my only grief, this nation alone rebellious against me, *contemptuous of my yoke* and stronger than my art" (Hughes, 16; italics mine). In order to combat the lordship of the "pius Jacobus," Milton's demon urges the Pope to deceit and treachery: "It is lawful to spread nets of any kind for heretics."

As the demonic plot moves forward, however, the Father, in a passage later to be echoed in *Paradise Lost*, looks down from Heaven and laughs at the desperate machinations of whose who would overcome truth; and finally the Father "...is willing to take upon himself the defense of his people's cause."

In 1626, Milton could still perceive the Will of God as upholding—and indeed intervening to preserve—the monarchy. If the "blest seed of *Terah's* faithful Son" had been the old Chosen People of God, the English—first under Elizabeth, then under James, and hopefully under James' successor of one year, Charles—were the new Elect Nation, the only nation against which the combined powers of Devil and Pope could avail naught, the only nation accepted by the Father as His People, and hence the repository of the true liberty resulting from righteous obedience to God's will. Because of their faithfulness in worshipping the "sacred deity of the true God," the English were preserved from a civil—and political—disaster, since part of the devil's instructions to the Pope was: "Then let the fierce Gaul or savage Spaniard attack them instantly, while they are panic stricken and stupefied by the catastrophe" (Hughes, 18). The English had correctly repudiated the religious heresies of the Marian monarchy; under James they were spared a return to the civil and religious disorders of the earlier period. With the discovery and destruction of the plot against James, the English were secured against both the religious tyranny of the Papists and the civil tyranny of foreign invaders.

"On the Death of a Fair Infant Dying of a Cough" (1628) has elicited much critical interest, in part because of its biographical connection to Milton's life and in part because of his unusual use of imagery and *topoi* more commonly associated with the Metaphysical poets. In fact, there seems little theological speculation in this poem so richly ornamented with classical allusions. Midway through the piece, he intrudes a momentary hesitance to accept the classical myths as truth, when he refers to "that high first-moving Sphere/Or …the Elysian fields (if such there were)" (39-40). Then he resumes his paean to the ancient gods, including an overt reference to Astraea. With her, Mercy and Truth enter the poem, providing a volta from classical to Christian reconciliation to death.

Having correlated the fair infant to the angels and created the image of her descending to earth and then quickly returning to Heaven as a model for human choice (stanza IX), Milton finally asks why the infant, in her natural innocence, did not remain on earth "to slake his wrath whom sin hath made our foe" (66), implicitly denying the doctrine of Original Sin and suggesting that human choice alone leads to perdition. Had she remained, he continues, her presence and her innocence would have turned back the ravages of plague then afflicting London. More to the point, she might have served, much as Lycidas will, as a mediator and guide for erring humanity, to "stand 'twixt us and our deserved smart" (69). In light of the image of the child's "heav'n-lov'd" innocence, *deserved* implies that we—humanity—have made false choices that merit punishment.

The great Nativity Ode ("composed 1629") is replete with suggestions of the importance of human choice. In the opening stanza, the Son "our deadly forfeit should release/And with his Father work us a perpetual peace" (6-7). *Work* implies volition on the part of the Son, a point emphasized in Stanza II, when Milton expressly states that the Son "laid aside" his divinity and "chose" to enter mortality (12, 14); later Milton notes that, in the image of Pan, He "kindly" descends to earth. *Kindly* here suggests both 'according to his Nature, to his kind' and 'graciously or generously', and both in turn indicate volition.

Within the Hymn itself, the stars refuse to depart until "their Lord himself bespake, and bid them go" (76); at his bidding—not commanding—they depart, taking with them their "stellar virtue" (*PL*, IV, 671). The Sun hides himself from the greater light of the Child (79-84). Only those who, according to tradition, had defied God and hence lost their freedom of action are compelled to movement. The pagan gods, sometimes interpreted as manifestations of the fallen angels, have no options; at the very presence of the Infant the "damned Crew," like the rebel angels during the War in Heaven, must perforce troop to Hell.

The Latin *Elegy VI*, written at roughly the same time as the Nativity Ode, touches upon choice, as has been noted above. The shift midway through from discussing elegy to a discourse on epic represents—whether seriously intended or facetious—a resolve to move from a lesser to a greater task. This task, Milton notes, requires more than intellectual commitment; it requires that the poet live worthily to function as a poet-priest. The maker of poetry is "sacred to the gods and is their priest" (Hughes, 52). The seriousness with which Milton took his poetic vocation throughout his life suggests that the choice, whether taken at the time the elegy was written or later, was crucial to his self-image as a poet.

In "L'Allegro" and "Il Penseroso" (c. 1631), Milton explicitly extends the question of freedom of choice into the universe of poetry. Critics frequently remark on the thematic and structural equality between the two poems and on the difficulty of determining conclusively which mode of living, if either, the poet might have been urging. The poems define apparently mutually exclusive moral choices which the speaker and, through him, the reader must make. The opening apotropaic "Hence" of each poem represents a decision to exclude one alternative and invite the second; and the closing lines reiterate that decision:

> Mirth, with thee I *mean* to live.
> ("*L'Allegro*," 152; italics mine)

> And I with thee *will choose* to live.
> ("Il Penseroso," 176; italics mine)

Part of the evidence for the superiority of the "Il Penseroso" mood is that the final volitive word in the first poem, *mean*, is itself a word of 'mean' or middle diction,[50] while "Il Penseroso" is resolved on a higher level of diction with *will choose*. Inclusive as they are of scenes and actions external to the poet, the twin poems relate not only to Milton's options but to the choices which each individual may make.

By the early 1630's, then, Milton had already responded in several ways to the general topic of liberty. In subsequent works, however, he probes beyond these surface meanings toward the most fundamental option, the possibility of man's aiding in his own regeneration. As early as "Upon the Circumcision" (1632-33) and "At a Solemn Music" (1633), Milton referred to fallen man's need to review and, when imperative, to revise choices in order to bring himself more fully into harmony with the perfect will of God.

"Upon the Circumcision" carefully contrasts two varying responses to the requirements of choice and liberty in Milton's poetic (and theological) universe—Christ's and man's. The invocation to the "flaming Powers, and winged Warriors bright" develops gradually but inexorably into a definition of the willing sacrifice (prefigured by the blood shed at the Circumcision) of the Son, by which he "bleeds to give us ease" (11). Humanity's participation in the sacrifice is essentially negative—that is, because of *our* willingness to transgress, Christ must suffer in our place:

> Alas, how soon our sin

---

[50] Cf. "Sonnet VII," l. 11; *Of Education, CPW*, II, 401.

> Sore doth begin
> His Infancy to seize!
>
> (12-14)

As he would later do in *Paradise Lost*, Milton emphasizes Christ's willingness to suffer, a willingness untainted by any hint of necessity but rather stemming from the unhindered outpouring of heavenly love for erring man: "Just law indeed, but more exceeding love!" The meeting of mercy and justice forms the volta of "Upon the Circumcision," just as the Incarnation and Passion were the great pivot in Christian history. The structure of the poem imitates the choices and reconciliation made by the Son.

If, however, Christ's circumcision represents an unselfish love founded upon divine love, humanity's choices (as outlined in the second half of the poem) represent the selfishness of sin and the constant necessity for individuals to re-make false choices. Milton recognizes the justice of God's judgments upon humanity, our "rightful doom remediless," a judgment caused initially by Adam's serious mischoice in Eden, continued by each individual in mortality, and overcome through the mercy of Christ's love:

> And that great Cov'nant *which we still transgress*
> Entirely satisfi'd,
> And the full wrath beside
> Of vengeful Justice bore for our excess....
>
> (21-24; italics mine)

Throughout this passage, Milton constantly reiterates the importance of free choice—both humanity's to fall and Christ's to redeem.

In "At a Solemn Music," on the other hand, Milton speaks of the role of the "Sphere-born harmonious Sisters, Voice and Verse," in reconciling the human with the divine. The power and influence of music is implicitly defined throughout the poem, although as might be expected that power is not expressed as an irresistible force, but rather as an aid to man's own imaginative perception of the divine. Music is

> Dead things with inbreath'd sense able to pierce,
> And to our high-rais'd fantasy present
> That undisturbed Song of pure concent,
> Aye sung before the sapphire-color'd throne
> To him that sits thereon,
> With Saintly shout and solemn Jubilee.
>
> (4-9)

Music is *able* to inspire, but man's own "high-rais'd fantasy" must work in conjunction with that inspiration. In the belief that through an awareness of the powers of "Voice and Verse" humanity might again participate in the harmony of the universe, Milton urges that

> ...we on Earth with undiscording voice
> *May* rightly answer that melodious noise;
> As once we did, till disproportion'd sin
> Jarr'd against nature's chime, and with harsh din
> Broke that fair music that all creatures made
> To their great Lord, whose love their motion sway'd
> In perfect Diapason, whilst they stood
> *In first obedience and their state of good.*
>
> (17-24; italics mine)

Music is *able* to inspire; man *may* respond. In his fallen state (the result of a conscious though erroneous choice), man is capable of a limited awareness and of limited choice among alternatives. Music thus becomes one means by which our "great Lord" might lead us back into the harmony which existed prior to Adam's "disproportion'd sin."

"At a Solemn Music" is an early statement of the theme underlying *Paradise Lost*, particularly in the latter books of the epic. Milton uses the imagery of music to suggest the process by which reconciliation between God and sinning man might be achieved. Man, through his own "harsh din," has disturbed universal harmony; through renewing his original song and willingly submitting to the ordering powers of music, man can repair his fault sufficiently to be reunited with Heaven. In his fallen state, man represents disharmony, multiplicity, and the limitations of time; by re-creating choices and choosing correctly to "answer that melodious voice," man may ultimately participate in harmony, unity, and eternity:

> O may we soon again renew that Song
> And keep in tune with Heav'n, till God ere long
> To his celestial consort us unite,
> To live with him, and sing in endless morn of light.
> (25-28)

The syntactic inversion of the penultimate line places the final responsibility for reconciliation and unification upon God, but man is nonetheless an active agent in the process. "At a Solemn Music," like "Upon the Circumcision," thus defines one means by which God allows man opportunities to re-make false choices and re-enter the proper path. In the first poem, Christ's Incarnation and Sacrifice satisfy for erring man the requirements of justice and make available to him the blessings of mercy; in the second, the wedding of Voice and Verse provides man's imagination with an image of the divine harmony of which man might ultimately be part.

ii. *Comus*

The interest in music as image of that universal harmony which underlies "At a Solemn Music" is equally explicit in Milton's long masque, *Comus* (1634). In the shorter poem, music is apostrophized as a means to the ultimate end of reconciliation of discordant humanity with God; in the masque, music becomes less the focus of discussion and more an integral part of a dramatic presentation which has as its stated purpose an explication of the force of virtuous choice in a fallen world. As the Attendant Spirit states in the opening passage of *Comus*, most are

> Unmindful of the crown that Virtue gives
> After this mortal change, to her true Servants
> Amongst the enthron'd gods on Sainted seats.
> Yet some there be *that by due steps* aspire

> To lay their just hands on that Golden Key
> That opes the Palace of Eternity:
> To such is my errand....
>
> (9-15; italics mine)

Initially, the Attendant Spirit introduces the reader to Comus by detailing the character's mythological genesis and history. Comus is the offspring of Bacchus and Circe, who, by appealing to the "intemperate thirst" of strangers, entices them to cast off reason by partaking of an enchanted drink:

> ...their human count'nance,
> Th' express resemblance of the gods, is chang'd
> Into some brutish form of Wolf, or Bear,
> Or Ounce, or Tiger, Hog, or bearded Goat,
> All other parts remaining as they were.
>
> (68-72)

Significantly, they do not *will* the change; instead it is imposed upon them, indicated by the passive form *is chang'd*.

As the Attendant Spirit retires from view, Comus enters with his rout, accompanied not by music, but by a "riotous and unruly noise," by "Midnight shout, and revelry" (103). The sense of musical harmony, control, and purpose which informed "At a Solemn Music" is entirely missing from Milton's treatment of Comus and his crew. The Lady, who has overheard Comus's singing, speaks of "Riot and ill-manag'd Merriment" and the "rudeness and swill'd insolence/Of such late Wassailers (172, 178-179). The kind of "music" represented by Comus well accords with his intentions, which include deceit, temptation and debilitation of reason and virtue, while it contrasts completely with the sorts of music other characters in the masque employ. The Lady, hearing the cacophony, implores "Sweet Echo,"

> So mayst thou be translated to the skies,
> And give resounding grace to all Heav'n's Harmonies.
>
> (242-243)

The Attendant Spirit succinctly defines the different kinds of music in *Comus* as he assumes the guise of Thyrsis and speaks to the Brothers, telling them how, seated on an ivy-covered bank, he had heard a "wonted roar" which

> ...fill'd the Air with barbarous dissonance,
> At which I ceas't, and listen'd them a while,
> Till an unusual stop of sudden silence
> Gave respite to the drowsy frighted steeds
> That draw the litter of close-curtain'd sleep;
> At last a soft and solemn-breathing sound
> Rose like a stream of rich distill'd Perfumes,
> And stole upon the Air, that even Silence
> Was took ere she was ware, and wish't she might
> Deny her nature, and be never more,
> Still to be so displac't. I was all ear,
> And took in strains that might create a soul
> Under the ribs of Death; but O ere long
> Too well I did perceive it was the voice
> Of my most honor'd Lady, your dear sister.
>
> (550-564)

The disruptive noise which characterizes Comus and his crew contrasts with the heartening, almost creative music of the Lady. License and virtue are thus paralleled to disharmony and harmony respectively. Music, which in "At a Solemn Music" was paramount, now serves as an image by which Milton might identify the moral natures of his characters. When the Attendant Spirit concludes the masque with a reference to the Music of the Spheres,

> Mortals that would follow me,
> Love virtue, she alone is free,
> She can teach ye how to climb
> Higher than the Sphery chime...,
>
> (1018-1021)

he reiterates that virtue, not music, is the subject of the masque.

Comus, of course, represents the antithesis of the virtue which Milton epitomizes in the Lady. If the Lady, surrounded as she is by references to song and harmony, represents adherence to virtue in the face of temptation, Comus and his raucous rout deny that virtue and choose instead license. As an image of the Circe-enchanter so common in Renaissance literature (and one must always remember Comus's parentage), Comus was, for Milton, particularly ominous in his advocacy of perverted reason. Comus's crew, a "rout of Monsters, headed like sundry sorts of wild beasts, but otherwise like Men and Women, their Apparel glistering," makes visual the consequences of false choice, of succumbing to the "intemperate thirst" which imbrutes men's reason and enslaves them to Comus's will.

The Lady, on the other hand, immediately suggests the virtue—identified initially as virginity, although ultimately fused with chastity—which Comus and his "damned crew" have denied. As Comus states, as he hushes his clamorous followers:

> Break off, break off, I feel the different pace
> Of some chaste footing near about this ground….
> (145-146)

Comus recognizes a difference between himself and the approaching Lady, and as she nears, he appeals to magic in order to deceive her and lead her more easily into embracing the proffered pleasures of his potion (153-156). From the sounds of her footsteps alone, Comus is able to perceive that the Lady will not easily succumb to him and therefore resorts to the deceitful guise of a "gentle Shepherd," a disguise which Milton will later parallel in Satan's assumption of the form of a Serpent in *Paradise Lost* and an "aged man in Rural weeds" in *Paradise Regained.* Upon seeing the Lady and hearing her soliloquy, Comus recognizes her innocence and determines to try it. Even though he feels that "Sure something holy lodges in that breast" (246), even though the Lady represents a virtue to which Comus almost intuitively responds before launching upon his stratagem of temptation, he nonetheless concludes, "I'll speak to her/And she shall be my Queen" (264-265).

The Lady is, indeed, initially deceived, her sight distorted. She is, however, ultimately armed against his deceit. Earlier, as she had become increasingly uneasy in the dark loneliness of the forest, she had expressed confidence in the sources of her strength: "...strong siding Champion Conscience," "pure-eye'd Faith, white-handed Hope," and the "unblemish'd form of Chastity." As if in confirmation of her faith in such protective powers, the Lady sees "a sable cloud/Turn forth her silver lining on the night" (223-224); the intrusion of light into the forest's darkness suggests that the Lady's confidence is at least in part warranted.

We can recognize in the Lady's trust, however, a preview of Eve in the Garden. Eve, too, felt secure in her Faith and Obedience; she, too, was surrounded by "glist'ring Guardian[s]" sent to ward off Satan, the "slavish [officer] of vengeance." In Eve's case, of course, the temptation was facilitated by her own choices previously entered into, particularly her decision to separate herself from Adam. The Lady, on the other hand, is alone in the forest because her brothers—not she—had made a choice, i.e., to step to a nearby thicket in search of berries or fruit for her, provided almost spontaneously for her benefit (185-187). In both episodes, however, Milton has carefully isolated his "lady" from the assistance of others in order that she might freely make her own choices.

Initially, the Lady's responses to Comus seems to foreshadow Eve's responses to the Serpent. Comus's speech of welcome resembles that by which Satan would later beguile Eve in *Paradise Lost*; the Lady is a "foreign wonder," a goddess of the wood. The fair and flattering speech deceives the Lady, who believes Comus's claim to have seen her brothers (which, like the Serpent's claim to have partaken of the fruit, is an outright lie) and accepts his offer to guide her through the forest maze. Eve falls through accepting the superficial reasoning of the Serpent; the Lady inadvertently places herself in Comus's power by accepting him as an honest shepherd, in which guise he presents himself to her:

> In a place
> Less warranted than this or less secure
> I cannot be, that I should fear to change it.

> Eye me blest Providence, and square my trial
> To my proportion'd strength. Shepherd lead on.
>
> (326-330)

Again, Milton has created a situation which he will later parallel in *Paradise Lost*. The Lady and Eve are both confronted by false guides who offer to conduct them through the forest—the Serpent promises to lead Eve to the Tree whose fruit has given him the power of speech; Comus promises to lead the Lady to the "green mantling vine" where her brothers are "Plucking ripe clusters." Neither Eve nor the Lady is yet fallen, but each has, by accepting the offer of her respective guide, made possible subsequent temptations. Eve's temptation is based largely on pride and appetite—is in fact internal—and she falls; the Lady's, on the other hand, is a more immediately physical temptation—perhaps *threat* might be a more appropriate term—and she remains true to the virtue which she represents.

As the Lady and Comus depart into the forest, the masque returns to the two brothers and their debate on the efficacy of innocent virtue in a fallen world. The brothers are perhaps too optimistic in their lack of concern for their sister. In his expression of worry for her, the Second Brother couches his speech in words adumbrative of Eve's temptation and fall in *Paradise Lost*:

> ...beauty, like the fair Hesperian Tree
> Laden with blooming gold, had need the guard
> Of dragon watch with unenchanted eye,
> To save her blossoms and defend her fruit
> From the rash hand of bold Incontinence.
> You may as well spread out the unsunn'd heaps
> Of Miser's treasure by an outlaw's den,
> And tell me it is safe, as bid me hope
> Danger will wink on Opportunity,
> And let a single helpless maiden pass
> Uninjured in this wild surrounding waste.
>
> (393-403)

This has in fact happened, even though the Elder Brother has earlier rejected the thought of any substantial danger (370). In answer to the Second Brother's speech, the Elder reveals the source of his optimism—the "sacred rays of Chastity" (425), which will surely draw Heaven down to the aid of threatened purity.

By the time Comus and the Lady reappear, then, Milton has established a pattern similar to that which he will employ decades later in describing the Fall of Man. The innocent Lady, entrapped and lost in the dark forest though she may be, is nonetheless capable and sufficient to withstand the temptation which the Second Brother foresees. If she is to fall, it will be through her own choices, even though the Elder Brother also indicates that when a soul is found sincerely chaste, the angels themselves will cooperate in restraining "sin and guilt" (455-456). The angels may—and do—prove inefficacious; the crux of the matter lies within the individual. Through proper choice, man may attain "The crown that Virtue gives/After this mortal change" (9-10); through improper choice, man must join with the imbruted forms of Comus's crew.

Milton avoids narrating the actual entrapment of the Lady. When the scene changes from the forest to the Palace of Comus, she is already seated in the alabaster chair. As the Second Brother had feared, Virtue is apparently in bondage to license and passion. Again, however, Milton's paradoxical approach to freedom allows the Lady, immobile and incapable of overt action, to assert her true freedom. As Comus boasts of having bound her, she responds:

> Fool, do not boast,
> Thou canst not touch the freedom of my mind
> With all thy charms, although this corporal rind
> Thou hast immanacl'd, while Heav'n sees good.
> (663-666)

Comus presents alternatives ostensibly fuller and wider than what he sees as mere abstinence, urging a perverted sort of magnanimity:

> Beauty is nature's coin, must not be hoarded,
> But must be current, and the good thereof

> Consists in mutual and partak'n bliss,
> Unsavory in th' enjoyment of itself.
>
> (740-743)

Against all his arguments and blandishments, the Lady remains sure in her dedication to virtue. She realizes—and through her the audience of *Comus* realizes—that true freedom depends first and foremost upon self-discipline and self-control, not upon intemperance and riotous indulgence. Hearing the Lady's speech and observing her dedication to the "sage/And serious doctrine of Virginity" (786-787), Comus feels his powers waning and experiences

> ...a cold shudd'ring dew [which]
> Dips me all o'er, as when the wrath of Jove
> Speaks thunder and the chains of Erebus
> To some of Saturn's crew.
>
> (802-805)

Rejecting this warning to desist in his temptation, Comus concludes his appeal to the Lady with four words: "Be wise and taste." At this point the Lady is physically at Comus's mercy. If he has not already made escape impossible, he has at least warned her against any attempts:

> Nay Lady, sit; if I but wave this wand,
> Your nerves are all chain'd up in Alabaster,
> And you a statue; or as Daphne was,
> Root-bound, that fled Apollo.
>
> (659-662)

The sexual threat implicit in Comus's reference to the Daphne/Apollo myth sufficiently suggests Comus's physical power over the Lady. Yet he seems incapable of moving overtly against her virtue, of forcing her to drink his potion. The challenge "Be wise and taste" thus not only effectively summarizes Comus's appeal to the Lady to deny her experiential knowledge and trust in knowledge claimed by another (and the specious arguments which Milton would later put into the mouths of the Serpent and of Eve), but also—and perhaps more importantly—defines Milton's respect for the independent choices upon which virtue depends. None of his tempters—Comus; Satan in *Paradise Lost* and *Paradise Regained*; the fallen Eve confronting Adam in *Paradise Lost*; Manoa, Dalila, Harapha, and the Public Officer in *Samson Agonistes*—is capable of forcing the tempted to deviate from virtue. Having voluntarily relinquished their own claims to virtue—in the cases of Satan and Eve, particularly—they are themselves constrained to give their victims at least a semblance of choice. Ultimately (as will be discussed in subsequent chapters) this necessity for freedom of choice in the face of temptation stems from Milton's conception of the freedom of choice enjoyed by the Father and, as a result of the Father's decrees, by all rational creatures.

Having shown through her defense of the "Sun-clad power of Chastity" that she has penetrated Comus's attempts at charming her judgment as he had before charmed her eyes (756-799), the Lady need not answer Comus's final challenge, and indeed does not. As Comus holds the potion out to her, the brothers rush in, dispel Comus and his rout, and attempt to release their sister from the entrapments of the enchanted alabaster Chair. Through her determination to preserve what Milton variously calls Virginity or Chastity, the Lady has withstood the temptation placed before her and has preserved her innocence in the face of imbruting passion.

She is, however, ultimately incapable of releasing herself from the spells which Comus used to bind her to the Chair. Even the Attendant Spirit, dispatched "by quick command from Sovran *Jove*" to protect the three travelers as they passed through the forest, cannot himself undo the evil which holds the Lady. The Lady, innocent and pure though she may be, is nonetheless in a world in which evil also abides. Unlike Adam and Eve in their prelapsarian state—and much less like the loyal angels—she cannot confront evil and remain totally unaffected by that evil. And, in the semi-pagan world of *Comus*, the Christian grace promised to repentant and enduring man in *Paradise Lost* and *Paradise Regained* is not available; there is no Christ, no mortal Son of God, to offer himself in ransom to set the Lady free.

Instead, the Spirit must call upon Sabrina, herself a virgin who, through her choice of death over ravishment of her fair innocence, "underwent quick immortal change,/Made Goddess of the river" (841-842). The Attendant Spirit expresses his confidence that Sabrina

> If she be right invok't in warbled Song,
> For maid'nhood she loves...will be swift
> To aid a Virgin, such as was herself,
> In hard-besetting need
>
> (854-857)

and to "unlock/The clasping charm and thaw the numbing spell." The Attendant Spirit, who is curiously ineffective as a guardian, fails to realize that since the Lady has never consciously succumbed to Comus's temptation (we assume he originally bound her in the chair through deceit), there is no need to unread the spells themselves. With a few drops of fountain water—representing pure nature, with a suggestion of baptism imagery—and the touch of her chaste hand, Sabrina—the personification of purity, chastity, and virtue obdurately preserved, even to the death—releases the Lady. The Lady and her brothers proceed to their father's palace, and with a final epilogue the masque concludes.

Comus, then, is in large measure concerned with temptations surrounding the Lady's perseverance in virtue. She is the central character, the one upon whom the responsibility of choice is most clearly placed, and as the final song suggests, concerning the Lady and her brothers,

> Heav'n hath timely tri'd their youth,
> Their faith, their patience, and their truth,
> And sent them here through hard assays
> With a crown of deathless Praise.
>
> (970-973)

In "At a Solemn Music," Milton had commented rather abstractly on human choice in terms of a restoration of the "melodious noise" first jarred by man; in *Comus* he not only uses human choice more directly as the pivot of the narrative itself, but also suggests that of all choices man might make, adherence to virtue is paramount. The masque thus not only represents the choices of the fictitious participants—the Lady, her brothers, the Attendant Spirit, Comus, Sabrina—but also an education in proper choice for the actors, their immediate audience, and ultimately for the reader.

In *Comus*, Milton first explores in depth the motivations for human choice. Perhaps it is a manifestation of Milton's own youth that the questions which *Comus* confronts and the answers which it gives are not fully as satisfying as those of *Paradise Lost*. In *Comus*, Milton puts his Lady in grave physical—as well as moral—danger, with consequences which not even her appointed guardian can completely forestall or reverse. In *Paradise Lost*, both the questions and the answers have become more complex. Adam and Eve are never in immediate physical danger, yet their choices seem more difficult than the Lady's. Nor, indeed, is there quite as painless a restoration to righteousness promised them. In both the masque and the epic, however, Milton clearly emphasizes the importance of the free choices his characters make. In each, man either limits or expands his alternatives through false or true choice. Human characters choose their guides and councilors—Eve follows the Serpent, Adam submits to Eve's rhetoric, and the Lady follows the specious Shepherd deeper into the forest rather than remaining to await her brothers' promised return.

In *Paradise Lost*, Milton's concern is to illustrate the first error in human history, the first faulty choice directing subsequent mankind away from Paradise and toward the fallen earth. In the masque, he explores the function of choice in a world already fallen and inhabited not only by the virtuous but also by the licentious and the brutish. The central figure in the world of *Comus* is the Lady, and through her actions and choices, Milton attempts a definitive model of virtue preserved through proper choice.

iii. Lycidas

The death of Edward King in 1637 provided Milton a further opportunity to examine the viability of human choice, particularly as choice relates—as it had in *Comus*—to attaining and preserving a virtuous state. The two speakers in *Lycidas* (the "uncouth Swain" of lines 1-185 and the Narrator of lines 186-193) each suggest ways in which human responses to alternatives affect growth into virtue. *Comus* had dealt with a world in which the Lady's dedication to Chastity had essentially provided her with immediate restoration of physical liberty; in *Lycidas*, Milton deals with a world in which death and corruption apparently prosper, while virtue—represented by Lycidas as poet and as priest—is destroyed.

Initially, *Lycidas* denies any sense of freedom of alternative. With the premature death of *Lycidas*, the Swain is impelled to act in an unanticipated and unwelcome situation and "with forc'd fingers rude" (4) attempt an elegy for the dead shepherd. The tone of the opening passage suggests that the Swain is conscious of his insufficiencies as a poet and would rather avoid—or at the least delay—the responsibility which had fallen to him; yet Lycidas

> ...must not float upon his wat'ry bier
> Unwept, and welter to the parching wind,
> Without the meed of some melodious tear.
> (12-14)

By the end of his song, however, the Swain has developed beyond his initial hesitation and, as described by the Narrator, willingly embraces his role as poet.

Jon S. Lawry has analyzed *Lycidas* as a series of three dialectics, each of which is ultimately resolved either into a new problem or into a final resolution of preceding conflicts. According to Lawry, the three sections of the poem present confrontations between the fallen world of life and the ideal world of poetry. Death, the evanescence of fame, and the injustice of ecclesiastical corruption intrude on the pastoral innocence which the Swain continually attempts to create until, in the final passages, he must reconcile himself to the reality of unjust death in a fallen world. Through an imagistic equation of Lycidas with Christ, the Swain unites his vision of the ideal pastoral with the realities of experience as only a Christian poet may. Death becomes understandable through the Christian paradox which Milton would later explore more fully in *Paradise Lost* and *Paradise Regained*; here, he concludes with the image of "*Lycidas*, sunk low, but mounted high,/Through the dear might of him that walk'd the waves" (172-173). By creating the poem and probing alternative modes of reconciling the experiential with the ideal, the Swain, and through him the reader, can accept not only the untimely death of Edward King but also less obvious manifestations of injustice and evil in the world.[51]

Lawry's analysis thus suggests that *Lycidas*, a poem frequently criticized for its digressiveness, is actually a unified statement of Milton's perceptions about the world, poetry, and death. Yet beyond this, *Lycidas* also indicates an increasing maturity and complexity in Milton's attitudes toward human choice. In the earlier poems, choice had been straight-forward and often immediately rewarded. The "Thunderer" protects James from conspiracy, almost in recognition of James's protection of true religion in England; Voice and Verse provide a model of true celestial harmony, in which man may share; the Lady, threatened with physical danger, is preserved through her dedication to Chastity. In those instances in which a moral choice had to be made, the situations were quite clear-cut—good versus evil, with good triumphant. In *Lycidas*, however, Milton confronts a more complex question: of what value is the decision to act virtuously when the world seems inimical to virtuous men and in fact allows their destruction.

From the first line of the monody, Lycidas is demonstrably superior to most men. He is without peer, as poet, scholar, and priest. He is one whom the nymphs should have saved from the "remorseless deep," whom the "Herald of the Sea," "Camus, reverend Sire," and

---

[51] Jon S. Lawry, "'Eager Thought': Dialectic in *Lycidas*," in *Milton: Modern Essays in Criticism*, ed. Arthur E. Barker (London: Oxford University Press, 1965), p. 112-124.

the "Pilot of the Galilean lake" each mourn as "gentle Swain," "dearest pledge," and the antithesis of the "Blind mouths" of the corrupt clergy. And yet Lycidas is the one whom death takes. In a sense Lycidas more closely resembles the "guiltless damsel" Sabrina who

> flying the mad pursuit
> Of her enraged stepdam Guendolen,
> Commended her fair innocence to the flood,
> (*Comus*, 829-831)

and who dies as a result of her commitment to virtue than he resembles the Lady preserved against all physical harms by the force of her Chastity. Each of the three dialectics which Lawry identifies thus not only concerns reconciliations between life and death, poetry and the world, pastoral idealism and experiential actuality, but also explores the validity of virtuous choice in the face of unjust death.

In the first section of *Lycidas* (1-84), the Swain seeks to reconcile himself to the intrusion of death into the pastoral world. Lycidas's death forces the Swain to contemplate his own "destin'd urn" and to question presuppositions which had before seemed inviolate. Through his grief, the Swain is led to question not only the efficacy of the pastoral deities (50-51, 56-60), but also the usefulness of poetry itself (64-66). At the instant of his deep despair, in contemplation of the "blind Fury with th'abhorred shears," who "slits the thin-spun life," the Swain receives the first answer to his questions: "But not the praise...." The virtuous man, here represented by *Lycidas* as poet, may be destroyed, removed from the world, but his Fame—and by extension his virtue and the consequences of his righteous choice—endures beyond the world (78-84).

In the second section of the poem (85-131), the Swain moves from questioning the fact of death in general to questioning the justness of Lycidas's death. He begins by returning once again to the pastoral mode, and, as the passage progresses, he discovers that the natural world was not in fact responsible for Lycidas's death. Contrary to the Swain's statements in the first section, the Ocean and winds are guiltless:

> It was that fatal and perfidious bark
> Built in th'eclipse and rigg'd with curses dark,
> That sunk so low that sacred head of thine.
>
> (100-102)

The suggestion that a man-made artifact was the instrument of Lycidas's death is followed by the revelation that *Lycidas* was not only the image of the virtuous man as poet but also an image of the virtuous man as scholar and priest. Camus, representing Cambridge University, and Peter, representing Lycidas's chosen vocation as priest, appear and dually mourn the loss of Lycidas and illustrate the vast differences between the virtuous Lycidas, whom death has taken, and the conspicuously evil men who enjoy life:

> They are sped;
> And when they list, their lean and flashy songs
> Grate on their scrannel Pipes of wretched straw.
> The hungry Sheep look up, and are not fed,
> But swoln with wind, and the rank mist they draw,
> Rot inwardly, and foul contagion spread....
>
> (122-127)

The Swain questions the usefulness of Lycidas's apparent commitment to virtue, when evil flourishes and virtue is destroyed. In answer to this question, Peter reveals that

> ...that two-handed engine at the door
> Stands ready to smite once and no more.
>
> (130-131)

Corruption may seem to prosper now, but in a Christian universe, evil—epitomized by false choice—will ultimately be punished.

In the final section of the poem, the Swain investigates the possibility that virtue will ultimately be rewarded. As the poem returns for the third time to pastoral images, the Swain goes beyond what he now perceives to be empty classical tropes and traditions and enters Christian pastoral. Only as a Christian poet can he understand the significance of Lycidas's excellence as poet, scholar, and priest. After the catalogue of flowers, each home-grown and native English, the Swain begins to speak of a Lycidas who strongly resembles *Comus*'s Sabrina:

> Weep no more, woeful Shepherds weep no more,
> For *Lycidas* your sorrow is not dead,
> Sunk though he be beneath the wat'ry floor,
> So sinks the day-star in the Ocean bed,
> And yet anon repairs his drooping head,
> And tricks his beams, and with new-spangled
> Ore, Flames in the forehead of the morning sky....
> (165-171)

Sabrina had voluntarily committed herself to the river to preserve her chastity; Lycidas had committed himself to virtue—as poet, scholar, and priest without peer—and now is dead. Yet like Sabrina (and perhaps the Fair Infant before her), he is not entirely lost to mortality but serves instead as the "Genius of the shore." He has been accepted into the

> ...blest Kingdom meek of joy and love.
> There entertain him all the Saints above,
> In solemn troops, and sweet Societies
> That sing, and singing in their glory move,
> And wipe the tears for ever from his eyes.
> Now *Lycidas*, the Shepherds weep no more;
> Henceforth thou art the Genius of the shore,
> In thy large recompense....
> (177-184)

Through the course of the monody, the Swain has confronted several essential questions, each dealing with Lycidas's relationship to his world. In the first section, the Swain contemplated the apparent helplessness of the gods of poetry in the face of death, and discovered that Fame can surmount death. In the second, he questioned why the virtuous man dies while the corrupt prosper, and he was told that finally evil will be punished—if not during this life, then later. And in the third, he discovered that through death, Lycidas is in fact exalted into a protector and guide to "all that wander in that perilous flood." If *Comus* in part suggested that virtue alone is capable of protecting man from inimical forces in the world, *Lycidas* suggests (to the Swain at least) that even though death and corruption have apparently overcome the virtues personified by Lycidas, those virtues are not finally destroyed.

In the Christian world of *Lycidas*, evil will be defeated and good rewarded, but the administration of such justice is not wholly a matter of this life. The Swain, then, has come to understand why Lycidas, the poet without peer, could be taken, while he, uncouth and unskilled, alone remains to sing his monody; why Lycidas, scholar and priest, might die, while lesser and more corrupt men survive and prosper. By so understanding, the Swain finally chooses to accept wholeheartedly the task which had fallen to him. As the Narrator concludes the poem, the Swain is no longer associated with "forc'd fingers rude," "Bitter constraint," or a heavy sense of compulsion. Instead,

> He touch't the tender stops of various Quills,
> With eager thought warbling his Doric lay....
> At last he rose, and twitch't his Mantle blue.
> Tomorrow to fresh Woods, and Pastures New.
> (188-189; 192-193)

There is a resemblance in tone and movement between this passage and the final lines of *Paradise Lost*. In each instance, Milton has progressed from despair and death to reconciliation and hope in promised blessings. *Lycidas* becomes in a sense a therapeutic experience, in which the Swain, like Adam and Eve in Book XII of *Paradise Lost*, discovers meaning in a universe which had seemed arbitrary, cruel, and threatening. He is now content to enter that world, aware not only of its dangers and pains, but also of its ultimate purposefulness and potential for fulfillment.

iv. The Prose

From 1640 until the publication of *Paradise Lost*, Milton was occupied primarily with prose which, although responding to specific stimuli, nonetheless relates directly to Milton's concern with liberty. Even in the few poems he complete during those years, however, the perennial theme of liberty surfaces, albeit usually tangentially. The two vituperative sonnets answering public response to *Tetrachordon*, for example, oppose civil liberty to license. The "Owls and Cuckoos, Asses, Apes, and Dogs" (XII, 4), like the general public who leave the pamphlet "seldom por'd on" (XI, 4), show by their behavior that they are neither "wise nor good" (XII, 12), disdaining the opportunity to strike for the domestic liberty implicit in Milton's relaxed attitude toward divorce. "On the New Forcers of Conscience" attacks a similar attitude, in which "Men whose Life, Learning, Faith, and pure intent" (9) are rewarded with the unjust label of "Heretics." Goodness and virtuous choice in service of the Commonwealth reap, not honor, but opprobrium. Certain individuals, however, remain true to their heritage of liberty; Fairfax (XV), Cromwell (XVI), and Vane (XVII) each exemplify virtuous choice in their labors for the Commonwealth. The "slaughter'd Saints (XVIII) of the Piedmont massacre deserve the name of Martyrs for their dedication to truth; while the poet himself, blind and seemingly unable to actively "serve" his Maker discovers that acceptance of God's will is sufficient labor, that "They also serve who only stand and wait" (XIX). Appropriately, the careful placement of *stand* adumbrates the Son's act of service to the Father, when on the Pinnacle of the Temple in *Paradise Regained,* he "stands" both literally and figuratively.

In the prose, on the other hand, he confronts the issue more overtly. In the *Second Defense of the English People*, Milton defines three sorts of liberty, particularly as each relates to his career as pamphleteer:

> Since, then, I observed that there are, in all, three varieties of liberty without which civilized life is scarcely possible, namely ecclesiastical liberty, do-

> mestic or personal liberty, and civil liberty, and since I had already written about the first, while I saw that the magistrates were vigorously attending to the third, I took as my province the remaining one, the second or domestic kind. (*CPW*, IV, 624)

Although Milton here justifies his involvement in such matters as marriage, education, and freedom of expression, his division of liberty in effect provides a tripartite guide to most of his prose writings, each of which confronts one of the three essential sorts. Milton's prose frequently responds to controversies paralleling the progress of reformation in England. Thus Milton's three liberties correspond to a concern shared by his contemporaries as the initial conflict—the question of church reformation—gradually expanded to include the critical issues of freedom of individual conscience and ideal civil liberty.

The first phase of Milton's career as pamphleteer was concerned with ecclesiastical matters. The titles of the early prose works clearly indicate Milton's interests: *Of Reformation Touching Church Discipline in England* (1641); *Of Prelatical Episcopacy* (1641); *Animadversions upon the Remonstrant's Defense against Smectymnuus* (1641); *The Reason of Church Government Urged against Prelaty* (1642); and *An Apology Against a Pamphlet Called "A Modest Confutation of the Animadversions upon the Remonstrant's Defense against Smectymnuus"* (1642). Each work confronts both the theological issues of the early years of the civil war and the question underlying the process of reformation—the relationship between reformation in the church and human liberty.

For Milton, as for many of his contemporaries, the problem of ecclesiastical liberty—and particularly of freedom from the onerous burdens of episcopacy—was a necessary preliminary to domestic and civil liberty. Man must first be freed to approach God in righteousness and truth before he may partake fully of the other external forms of liberty; and during the early 1640's, Milton—along with concourses of others in England—was convinced that such freedom was near. Through the labor of himself and others like him, Milton argues, truth would be brought to the fore, and

> the property of truth is, where she is publicly taught, to unyoke and set free the minds and spirits of a nation first from the thralldom of sin and superstition, after which all honest and legal freedom of civil life cannot be long absent.... (*Reason,* Hughes, 685)

Between 1643 and 1645, Milton's pamphlets related almost exclusively to the second element of his triad of liberties—domestic. During the three years in question, Milton published six pamphlets: *The Doctrine and Discipline of Divorce* (1644); *Of Education* (1644); *The Judgment of Martin Bucer concerning Divorce* (1644); *Areopagitica* (1644); *Tetrachordon* (1645); and *Colasterion* (1645). Critics have long noted that Milton's marriage to Mary Powell had a serious effect on the poet, so serious perhaps as to lead him to publish the first divorce tract, in which he argues urgently for freedom of conscience in marriage. Other—and perhaps more fundamental—reasons also explain Milton's shift in emphasis to a new form of liberty. Milton's conviction of his own worth and the worth of his beliefs compelled him into arguments by which he could show the necessity for each individual to be allowed the domestic liberty which the 1643-1645 pamphlets primarily defined.

Between 1645 and 1649, Milton published only an edition of his poetry (1645). In February of 1649, however, he again began publishing prose works. This time he was less interested in ecclesiastical or domestic liberty than in the third form, civil liberty. With the triumph of the Puritan forces apparently in sight, and the King on trial for his life, Milton foresaw the ultimate establishment of true civil liberty in England. Beginning then with the publication of *The Tenure of Kings and Magistrates* (1649), preceding by a matter of weeks his appointment as Secretary of Foreign Tongues to the Council of State under Cromwell, Milton dedicated his talents to defining and championing civil liberty.

With few exceptions, everything he published between 1649 and the restoration of Charles II in 1660 addressed itself to the state, either as a defense for civil policies or as an attempt to sway the erring (in Milton's mind, at least) English Commonwealth back onto its proper course. Within eleven years, he published *The Tenure of Kings and Magistrates* (1649); *Observations upon the Articles of Peace* (1649); *Eikonoclastes* (1649); *Johannis Miltoni, Angli, pro populo Anglicano defensio contra Claudii Salmasii defensionem regiam* (1651); *Johannis Miltoni, Angli, pro populo Anglicano defensio secunda* (1654); *Johannis Miltoni, Angli, pro se Defensio* (1655); *A Treatise of Civil Power* (1657); *A Letter to a Friend, Concerning the Ruptures of the Commonwealth* (1659); *The Ready and Easy Way to Establish a Free Commonwealth* (1660); and *The Present Means, and brief Delineation of a Free Commonwealth* (1660).

Arthur E. Barker cites the author of *Regii Sanguinis Clamor Ad Coelum* as claiming that Milton had "passed from the severing of marriages to the divorce of kingdoms," and then notes, concerning the majority of Milton's prose works between 1645 and 1660, that "the political pamphlets did in fact apply to a larger field the ideas developed in the divorce tracts."[52] The divorce tracts, in turn, had developed from Milton's concerns in the earlier anti-Prelatical tracts. Milton had investigated each of his three major divisions of liberty consecutively, and in each instance he had discovered that the inherent liberty of the individual provided the underlying rationale for his theory of freedom. In opposing prelacy, he urged the right of individual Christians to participate in the controversy; in defending domestic liberty, he argued for individual conscience as the guideline in private matters; and in defending civil liberty, he had urged the rights and responsibilities of the Christian civil community. As early as *Of Reformation* (1641), he had emphasized the importance of individual freedom of choice when, in speaking of civil governments, he had defined them in terms of individuals:

> that which is good, and agreeable to monarchy, will appear soonest to be so, by being good, and agreeable to the true wel-fare of every Christian, and that which can be justly prov'd hurt full, and offensive to every true Christian, wil be evinc't to be alike hurtful

---

[52] Arthur E. Barker, *Milton and the Puritan Dilemma*, (Toronto: University of Toronto Press, 1942), p. 123.

> to monarchy: for God forbid, that we should separate and distinguish the end, and good of a monarch, from the end and good of a monarchy, or of that, from Christianity. (*CPW*, I, 572-573)

Milton's opinions of monarchy were to change radically by 1660, but his initial emphasis on individual liberty in all three spheres—ecclesiastical, domestic, and civil—remained intact.

Through the early works, then, Milton returns again and again to the themes of liberty and freedom, in political, personal, and theological senses. His concern for freedom of will and choice is aptly summarized in a short passage from the *Second Defense*:

> know then that to be free is the same thing as to be pious, to be wise, to be temperate and just, to be frugal and abstinent, and lastly, to be magnanimous and brave; so to be the opposite of all these is the same as to be a slave. (Hughes, 837)

True choice is open-ended, false choice narrows alternatives, enslaves man to the license that he has misconstrued as liberty. Freedom is not gratuitously extended to man, especially since the loss of Eden. Right reason and proper choice are the implements by which to forge all liberty and simultaneously the goals of humanity and, in a larger sense, of all creatures capable of thought, rationality, and choice.

v. Summation

Underlying the early poems and the prose tracts, then, is the sense that man must ultimately be free to make the choices required of him by life. Man cannot yet stand independent of any external aid, as Milton explicitly states in the *Treatise of Civil Power*:

> If then both our beleef and practice, which comprehend our whole religion, flow from faculties of the inward man, free and unconstrainable of themselves

> by nature, and our practise not only from faculties endu'd with freedom but from love and charitie besides, incapable of force, and all these things by transgression lost, but renewed and regenerated in us by the power and gift of God alone; how can such a religion as this admit of force from man...? (*CPW*, VII, p. 256)

Man is, however, capable of bearing responsibility for his actions and of learning to choose correctly. Choice, for Milton, is still viable, even though individuals must make those choices in a fallen and imperfect world. As he asserts in a justly famous passage from the *Areopagitica,*

> many there be that complain of divin Providence for suffering *Adam* to transgresse, foolish tongues! when God gave him reason, he gave him freedom of choice, for reason is but choosing; he had bin else a meer artificiall *Adam*, such an *Adam* as he is in the motions. (*CPW*, II, p. 527)

Adam, as Milton will subsequently demonstrate in *Paradise Lost,* is far more than a mere puppet.

Milton's definition of liberty in the *Second Defense* thus gives us a clue to his attitudes toward liberty and choice before 1660. Yet in an important sense, his division of liberty into three external manifestations is somewhat misleading, since each of the varieties assumes the predominance of internal liberty. Each of the three liberties is formally opposed to those

> new foes' [which] arise
> Threat'ning to bind our souls with secular chains...

and against which foes Milton appeals to the leaders of his day,

> Help us to save free Conscience from the paw
> Of hireling wolves whose Gospel is their maw.

(Sonnet XVI, 11-12, 13-14)

As Milton himself clearly states, however, both in the *Second Defense* and later in *Paradise Lost* (XII, 585-587), true liberty is not merely that manifested in ecclesiastical, domestic, or civil relationships between men, but rather that which must be "sought from within than from without, and whose existence depends not so much on the terror of the sword as on sobriety of conduct and integrity of life" (Hughes, 830). Each variety of liberty thus depends upon a more fundamental liberty, upon an internal, immutable freedom of choice, an awareness of essential alternatives and a freedom to choose between them. Basic to any sense of political, ecclesiastical, or domestic liberty is the deeper sense of man as an agent free to make choices.

Milton's liberty, in all of its manifestations, schematically resembles a series of concentric circles. The outer circle represents civil liberty, that freedom which includes all members of the polity; within that circle is a smaller one representing ecclesiastical or Christian liberty, that freedom which includes all members of the society of the regenerate; and within that, a smaller circle which represents domestic liberty, the freedom of man to function within his family and as an individual. The smallest circle, and the one central to each of the others, is individual liberty; each individual stands in direct confrontation with the will of God and may choose to obey or not. The choice within this smallest, most intensely personal circle will determine each person's responses to each of the other forms of liberty. Only through virtuous choice at this level is liberty possible in any form. As Milton states in the *Tenure of Kings and Magistrates,* "indeed, none can love freedom heartilie but good men; the rest love not freedom but licence..." (*CPW,* III, p. 190)

Ultimately, then, all liberty—at least according to Milton's definition in the *Second Defense*—is built upon the freedom which emerges through and manifests itself in a life of virtuous choice. Milton adamantly believed that all individuals possessed this liberty, whether they recognized it or not; and even more importantly, Milton's universe, as defined in the prose and the poetry, is one in which freedom of choice persists as an essential characteristic. The rights and responsibilities of liberty and choice fall equally throughout the universe, from God—the Fountainhead of all righteousness—to fallen man, who may, after constant labor and striving, assist through faith in his own redemption. From the Father, through the Son, the angels (both unfallen and fallen), and finally humanity, the links of freedom and responsibility reach out to reunite a universe jarred and made disharmonious through false choice.

CHAPTER THREE

The Father—
Fountainhead of Moral Freedom

> No man who knows ought can be so stupid to deny that all men naturally were borne free, being the image and resemblance of God himself....
> —*Tenure of Kings and Magistrates*

Milton exemplifies the conflict between the optimistic Renaissance vision of man as an embryonic deity whose will is sufficient for exaltation and the more pessimistic Reformation view of man as less than nothing in the presence of an all-powerful God. Milton reconciled this conflict primarily through a belief in an ultimately unknowable God and the conclusion that attaining a conviction of God's existence is essential to the progress of man. Emulating God—as far as is humanly possible—is the fundamental purpose of all human knowledge:

> The end then of learning is to repair the ruins of our first parents by regaining to know God aright, and out of that knowledge to love him, to imitate him, to be like him, as we may the neerest by possessing our souls of true vertue, which being united to the heavenly grace of faith makes up the highest virtue. (*Of Education, CPW*, II, 366-367)

If by exercising aright his freedom of choice man is indeed imitating God, being like Him, then at no point could a discussion of moral freedom in Milton's writings more appropriately begin than by defining the freedom of choice which Milton's God possesses.

Milton recognized the impossibility of adequately defining the nature of God. His disparagement of theological systems in the opening paragraphs of *The Christian Doctrine* illustrates his impatience with those who claimed complete understanding of God. He did not, however, despair of knowing enough to rely upon his faith in the existence and purposes of God. God has accommodated Himself and His nature to the understanding of men, at least enough for individuals to adhere to the revelations of the Scriptures. From the Scriptures, humanity learns much about the Deity; from them alone may any justifiable conclusions about Him be drawn:

> We ought not to imagine that God would have said anything or caused anything to be written about himself unless he intended that it should be a part of our conception of him. On the question of what is or what is not suitable for God, let us ask for no more dependable authority than God himself. (*CD*, I, ii, p. 134)[53]

Milton rarely explored the specific nature of the Father. In general, Milton's God remains ineffable, dark with His excessive brightness. This is not to suggest that Milton never attempted to define the *attributes* of God. *The Christian Doctrine* isolates nine fundamental attributes of the Father—Truth, Spirit, Immensity and Infinity, Eternity, Immutability, Incorruptibility, Omnipresence, Omnipotence, and Unity (*CD*, I, ii, 139-152)—since in order to resolve questions of the source and nature of evil, as Milton's theodicy attempted, the poet was forced to assign specific traits and qualities to the Father.

---

[53] All references to *The Christian Doctrine* are from Kelley's edition in the *CPW*, VI.

In addition to listing these traits, however, Milton refers again and again in *The Christian Doctrine* to yet another attribute of the Father, His absolute freedom of choice. Early in the treatise, Milton writes that in His GENERAL DECREE, God has "ABSOLUTE FREEDOM: that is, not forced, not impelled by any necessity [*nulla necessitate impulsus*], but just as he wished." God's decrees are based on "absolute freedom...absolute wisdom and...absolute holiness" (*CD*, I, iii, 154, 153).

As a consequence of his emphasis on God's freedom, Milton is forced to deny Aristotle's *Actus Purus,* or "pure actuality," since otherwise the Deity could do only that which necessity required and would not be free (*CD,* I, iii, 145-146). For Milton, only God is capable of acting on *whatever* He wills with absolute freedom. God's choices, based as they are on complete foreknowledge, are invariably righteous and perfect, while man's stubborn will possibly—if not probably—diverts him from the intentions of God (*CD,* I, iii, 159).

Unlike man's dependence upon external circumstances, which in part determine his alternatives, God's freedom functions unimpaired in all circumstances. If any action fails to achieve His purposes, God may simply forbid it. In Book I of *Paradise Lost*, for example, Milton asserts that Satan rose from the burning lake of Hell only because

> the will
> And high permission of all-ruling Heaven
> Left him at large to his own dark designs,
> That with reiterated crimes he might
> Heap on himself damnation, while he sought
> Evil to others, and enrag'd might see
> How all his malice serv'd but to bring forth
> Infinite goodness, grace and mercy shown
> On Man by him seduc't....
>
> (*P.L.*, I, 211-219)

The reader should not be deceived by the posturing of Satan and his legions, bright as the fallen Archangel might seem to shine against the darkness palpable of Hell and later of Pandemonium. Milton carefully reminds the reader that above Satan's falsity and demonic arrogation of monarchy, the Father's will continues undisturbed—indeed, Satan's seduction of man will bring about a foreseen conclusion desired by the Father.

Later, as Satan and Gabriel are about to battle in Book IV, the Father (like His Homeric counterpart) weighs the combatants in His Golden Scale and finds Satan wanting. At this Gabriel addresses his antagonist:

> Satan, I know thy strength, and thou know'st mine,
> Neither our own but giv'n; what folly then
> To boast what Arms can do, since thine no more
> Than Heav'n permits, nor mine, though doubl'd now
> To trample thee as mire.
> (*P.L.*, IV, 1006-1010)

Although this passage may seem to imply that God simply imposes His will upon all lower creatures, without any regard for their liberty, Milton continuously reminds the reader that God's perfect foreknowledge precedes His decrees. God foreknows what Satan and his infernal crew will devise, just as He foreknows that Gabriel and Satan will not engage in personal combat. God's foreknowledge, not internal necessity, justifies the Father's decision to allow certain actions in the first episode and to deny others in the second.

In the affairs of men, the Father likewise does not necessitate; He foreknows perfectly and thus enjoys absolute freedom of righteous choice. The divine plan, of which the fall of Adam and Eve constitutes an essential part, rests not upon force and necessity but upon choice, wisdom, and a perfect freedom which God extends to all rational creatures:

> God has complete foreknowledge, so he knows what men, who are free in their actions, will think and do, even before they are born.... (*C.D.*, I, ii, 150)

And as with men, so also with angels both loyal and rebellious.

The Father is not restricted, however, by the choices of men and other creatures. Milton's God is immutable, regardless of the vast freedom which He bestows upon man, since the choices He allows inferiors are not absolute and eternal decrees but rather matters "where God has made man his own master" (*C.D.*, I, iii, 161). The Father does not force; He allows humanity the freedom He enjoys, although since humans are both fallen and imperfect their abilities to employ that freedom remain limited. The Father's standards are correct and eternal, and as the Son states in *Paradise Lost*,

> ...Father, [thou] art Judge
> Of all things made, and judgest only right.
> (*P.L.*, III, 154-155)

God's creative goodness is absolutely "free to act or not" (*P.L.*, VII, 171-172) and depends only upon His omniscience and perfection.

More fundamentally, since the Father has complete freedom of choice, nothing compels Him to exclude the evil consequences of choices entered into by His creatures; after all, God extends to them the same freedom which He enjoys. Still, there are necessary limitations on God's power; Milton states that, since God did not create the universe out of nothing, no created thing can be "finally annihilated." Milton notes that not only is there no intimation of such annihilation in the Scriptures, but also that

> there are other reasons, besides that which has been just alleged, and which is the strongest of all, why this doctrine should be altogether exploded. First, because God is neither willing, nor properly speaking, able to annihilate anything altogether.[54]

Milton's assessment of God as in certain restricted senses limited—that is, if He is incapable of annihilating "anything altogether," He is not absolutely omnipotent—is not entirely a product of Milton's own theological speculations. Some Church Fathers had occasion-

---

[54] Cited in Conklin, pp. 71-72.

ally intimated that the Father might in some ways be limited. Origen, for example, argued that

> As no one can be a father without having a son, nor a master without possessing a servant, so even God cannot be called omnipotent unless there exists those over whom He may exercise His power, and therefore, that God may be shown to be almighty, it is necessary that all things should exist.[55]

Origen further stated that "God cannot do anything which is contrary to reason, or contrary to Himself." Milton would later echo that conclusion by stating that "The power of God is not exerted in things which imply a contradiction."[56]

Among Milton's contemporaries, parallel conceptions of a semilimited God were fairly common. In his preface to *The True Intellectual System of the Universe* (1678), Ralph Cudworth restricted both the nature and the freedom of God:

> *...all things do not Float without a* Head *and* Governour; *but there is an* Omnipotent Understanding Being Presiding *over all*: *That this* God, *hath an* Essential Goodness *and* Justice, *and that the differences of* Good *and* Evil, Morall, Honest, *and* Dishonest, *are not by mere* Will *and* Law *onely, but by* Nature, *and consequently, That the* Deity *cannot* Act, Influence, *and* Necessitate *men, to such things as are in their* Own Nature, Evil....[57]

Benjamin Whichcote similarly defined God as partially finite. After distinguishing between the Father's secret will and His revealed

---

[55] Harry F. Robins, *If This Be Heresy* (Urbana, Illinois: The University of Illinois Press, 1963), p. 65.

[56] Curry, p. 44; Robins, p. 95.

[57] Cudworth, *The True Intellectual System* (London, 1678; facsimile rpt. Stuttgart-Bad Cannstatt: Friedrich Fromann Verlag, 1964).

will, Whichcote asserted that the divine will, in either of its manifestations, is limited by Goodness. Consequently, only God is certain because in Him and in Him alone the will and the good agree perfectly: "God only can say He will, because He will in view of the complete agreement of His will and the right." James D. Roberts summarizes Whichcote's assertion that before

> the existence of evil, God does what infinite wisdom directs or goodness moves to prevent it, by declaring against it, by warning and admonishing, by frustration, and cross-providence. Subsequent to evil He brings good out of evil according to His goodness and pleasure.[58]

There is no suggestion that the Father desires to force acquiescence to the good.

Milton's view of the Father allows for similar self-imposed limits on the part of the Father, particularly as He appears in *Paradise Lost*. God warns, urges, and admonishes but refuses to interfere with the working-out of human or angelic freedom (III, 80-216). As He argues the need for a Redeemer, the Father clearly establishes the fact that He will in no way interpose to forestall forcibly the fall of man:

> I made [man] just and right,
> *Sufficient to have stood, though free to fall.*
>
> ...they themselves decreed
> Thir own revolt, not I: if I foreknew,
> Foreknowledge had no influence on their fault,
> Which had no less prov'd certain unforeknown.
>
> I form'd them free, and free they *must* remain,
> Till they enthrall themselves: I else *must* change

---

[58] James D. Roberts, Sr., *From Puritanism to Platonism in Seventeenth Century England* (The Hague: Martinus Nijhoff, 1968), pp. 78, 96.

> Thir nature, and revoke the high Decree
> Unchangeable, Eternal, which ordain'd
> Thir freedom: they themselves ordain'd thir fall.
> (*PL*, III, 98-99, 116-119, 124-128; italics mine)

And to "render Man inexcusable," the Father "sends Raphael to admonish him of his obedience, his free estate, and of his enemy near at hand; who he is, and why his enemy, and whatever else may avail Adam to know" (*PL*, V, "The Argument"). Never, however, would the Father force Adam's obedience.

Milton stresses the Father's wisdom, omnipotence, and freedom, while at the same time restricting the Father's omnipotence in those areas which are contradictions, using as proof texts II Timothy 2:13, Titus 1:2, and Hebrews 6:18 (*CD*, I, ii, 146). In *Paradise Lost*, Adam argues for the Father's partial limitation by questioning,

> Can [God] make deathless Death? that were to make
> Strange contradiction, which to God himself
> Impossible is held, as Argument
> Of weakness, not of Power.
> (X, 798-801)

Adam's postlapsarian responses to the Father's omnipotence are perhaps not wholly accurate, but they do concur with Milton's treatment of the Father elsewhere. Milton must demonstrate that God cannot decree all actions inevitably, since otherwise God becomes responsible for the sins which He foresees will soon overtake man. In order to avoid a tedious "schoolmaster God," Milton must amplify man's freedom of action to include initiating his own sin. God becomes limited insofar as some decrees remain contingent upon choices exercised by others.

In *Paradise Lost* as well as in *The Christian Doctrine* (the two works in which Milton most fully explores the Deity and His attributes), the poet presents a God who has absolute foreknowledge but who does not necessitate as a result of that foreknowledge:

> nothing happens because God has foreseen it, but rather he has foreseen each event because it is the result of particular causes which, by his decree, work quite freely and with which he is thoroughly familiar. (*CD,* I, iii, 164)

This God seems limited. Having decreed unalterably the free will of man, He is incapable of contravening that freedom. Milton justifies this attribute of the Father in Book III of *Paradise Lost,* in which the Father explains His decision to respect absolutely man's freedom of choice:

> Not free, what proof could they have giv'n sincere
> Of true allegiance, constant Faith or Love,
> Where only what they needs must do, appear'd,
> Not what they would....
>
> (103-106) [59]

Evil and sin result from man's freedom, not from God's decrees. A Deity characterized by such limitations is not in essence limited, however, since true freedom consists in choosing from among righteous alternatives; only license (as Milton understood it) enslaves rather than liberates. Absolute and perfect freedom must, paradoxically, restrict and limit itself, just as creation restricts and limits chaos. Only by participating in those restricted and limited alternatives can choice lead to liberty instead of to enslavement within self.

Given Milton's view of God, then, William Empson feels justified in concluding, with evident distaste, that "to achieve the fall of man was the mysterious purpose of God."[60] If divine foreknowledge is perfect and complete, then God knew in advance of the fall and purposely permitted the introduction of evil into His newly created world. Empson's challenge reflects still-persistent questions in Milton studies and in the wider arena of Christian apologetics—the whence and why of evil. Lactantius confronted evil as somehow im-

---

[59] See also *Areopagitica, CPW,* II, 514-515, 527.
[60] "Heaven's Awful Monarch," *Listener,* 64 (1960), pp. 111-112.

portant, if not essential, to human development, as a "part of God's deliberate choice for man's spiritual environment, a necessity for the very existence of a moral nature."[61] In a similar vein, the *Carmen de Providentia Divina,* attributed to Prosper of Aquitaine, while not defending evil as a deliberately introduced factor in human existence, does suggest indirectly that evil, though brought about by man, is fundamental to man's progress, since sin is a result of exercising (albeit inappropriately) the freedom granted to man at his creation. Through the abuse of freedom man brings about his present misery.[62] To this statement Milton would add that through repentance—that is, through a return to proper choice in the face of renewed temptation—man may participate in his own regeneration.

The possibility of choosing evil alternatives over good thus lies at the heart of Milton's conception of regeneration. The Father, possessing perfect freedom and inviolable justness in His choices, has freely given His rational creatures a similar freedom and responsibility (*CD*, I, iii, 160). Mary Ann Nevins Radzinowicz refers to this gift when she states that "the mercy of providence can be no other than permitting parallel choices," i.e., toward regeneration or toward hardening of the heart.[63] Nor does divine foreknowledge influence choices made by others:

> They [man] therefore as to right belong'd,
> So were created, nor can justly accuse
> Thir maker, or thir making, or thir Fate;
> As if Predestination over-rul'd
> Thir will, dispos'd by absolute Decree
> Or high foreknowledge; they themselves decreed
> Thir own revolt, not I ...

---

[61] Kathleen Ellen Hartwell, *Lactantius and Milton* (Cambridge, Massachusetts: Harvard University Press, 1929), p. 23.

[62] Evans, p. 113.

[63] Mary Ann Nevins Radzinowicz, "Eve and Dalila: Renovation and the Hardening of the Heart," in *Reason and Imagination: Studies in the History of Ideas, 1660-1800*. Ed. J. A. Mazzeo (New York: Columbia University Press, 1962), p. 158

> So without least impulse or shadow of Fate,
> Or aught by me immutably foreseen,
> They trespass, Authors to themselves in all
> Both what they judge and what they choose; for so
> I form'd them free, and free they must remain,
> Till they enthrall themselves....
>
> (*PL*, III, 111-117, 120-125)

Through this gift of freedom, of "permitting parallel choices," the Father is able not only to exalt those who choose correctly but also to exploit evil—notably that of Satan in *Paradise Lost*—and expedite the fulfillment of His desires for the righteous. God will not—cannot—work against the freedom He has decreed immutably for others, since if He did so,

> He would be mutable, and his intention would not be stable, if by a second decree he thwarted the freedom he had once decided upon, or cast the least shadow of necessity over it.
> From the concept of freedom, then, all idea of necessity must be removed. (*C.D.*, I, iii, 161)

God must then use the sin and evil entered into by lesser creations as tools by which to reverse and transmute themselves into goodness.

The power of God to allow "parallel choices" resolves a persistent exegetical problem: the purpose of the questions which God addressed to Adam and Eve after their fall:

> To begin with, His questions to the fallen pair seemed to imply that He was not omniscient, that he had to exact a confession before He knew what crime had been committed. The Rabbis consequently took some pains to point out that the Deity's ignorance was only apparent; He was really offering the sinners the opportunity to repent....[64]

---

[64] Evans, p. 52.

Evans's interpretation of the episode corresponds to Milton's. In confronting the sinning pair, the Father places the responsibility for confession, for repentance, and ultimately for forgiveness upon them. After reiterating to the Son that the culpability for the fall rests with man,

> no Decree of mine
> Concurring to necessitate his Fall,
> Or touch with lightest moment of impulse
> His free Will, to her own inclining left
> In even scale,
>
> (*PL*, X, 43-47)

the Father instructs the Son to descend to Paradise and judge the sinners. In answer to the questions posed by Son (who functions as an emissary of the Father and thus is fully aware of the fact of disobedience and fall), Adam shifts the blame for his decision onto Eve:

> This Woman whom thou mad'st to be my help,
> And gav'st me as thy perfet gift, so good,
> So fit, so acceptable, so Divine,
> That from her hand I could suspect no ill,
> And what she did, whatever in itself
> Her doing seem'd to justify the deed;
> Shee gave me of the Tree, and I did eat.
>
> (*PL*, X, 137-143)

Eve in turn looks to another for ultimate responsibility:

> The Serpent me beguil'd and I did eat.
>
> (*PL.*, X, 162)

Through the foreknowledge granted him by the Father, the Son knows the answer to his questions before they are asked. Adam and Eve fail this test when they deny their responsibility for their actions and for the consequences of their acts. Only later, when they symbolically return to the scene of judgment, do they turn from sin and seek forgiveness. Their "prostrate fall" to repentance, quite unlike their earlier fall into pride, stems from humility and results in an ascent to unity with God, achievable only through their reversal of an earlier mischoice. Their evil—willed and chosen by them and subsequently freely repudiated by them without external necessity—thus becomes an instrument by which Adam and Eve recognize their dependence upon the Father and by which the Father is able to restore them to righteousness.

Milton's God, then, represents the perfect state of freedom and moral liberty. He is Himself the Absolute, unhampered by superior decrees or edicts, relieved of any necessity for action, and limited only insofar as He cannot contradict His own decrees. Among His decrees, one of the most important is that which endows all rational beings, from the Son to created man, with reflections of the Father's own freedom, to be used or abused as the inner strength of each individual allows. In His own freedom, the Father never fails to consider the lesser but still essential freedom of all.

After thus defining the freedom of the Father, Milton was left with yet one difficulty: to illuminate the tension between the created beings' will to choice and the Creator's will to righteousness. This tension provides the impetus and motivation for the dramatic crises which the poet continually confronts.

CHAPTER FOUR

The Son—
Paradigm of Righteous Choice

> I who erewhile the happy Garden sung,
> By one man's disobedience lost, now sing
> Recover'd Paradise to all mankind,
> By one man's firm obedience fully tried
> Through all temptation....
> —*Paradise Regained*, I, 1-5

i. The Nature of the Son

In *The Christian Doctrine*, Milton emphasizes the *oneness* of God the Father as Absolute, an emphasis which buttresses the antitrinitarianism which many, if not most, critics have found evident in the prose and poetry. Milton's definition of God effectively precludes belief in a Trinity, since God cannot be both *one* and *not one*:

> Certainly the Israelites under the law and the prophets always understood that God was without question numerically one, and that there was no other beside him, let alone any equal to him. (*CD*, I, ii, 147-148)

It is difficult to date precisely alterations in Milton's view of the Godhead. A passage from the Nativity Ode,

> That glorious Form, that Light insufferable,
> And that far-beaming blaze of Majesty
> Wherewith he wont at Heav'n's high Council-Table,
> To sit the midst of Trinal Unity,
> He laid aside...,
>
>   (9-13)

implies an orthodox Trinity. Kelley has adduced that two references—the invocation to the "one Tripersonall GODHEAD" in *Of Reformation* (1641) and the mention of the Son as the "ever-begotten Light" in the *Animadversions* (1641)—suggest orthodoxy, with the first elements of antitrinitarianism appearing in the *Defensio pro Populo Anglicano* (1651). In general, however, Kelley concludes that references to the Godhead are fairly ambiguous from 1641 until the Picard draft of *The Christian Doctrine* (1660), which contained the antitrinitarian beliefs of the manuscript as finally published.[65]

Regardless of any attempts at precise dating, however, it is apparent that the poet's views of the relationship between Father and Son were unorthodox by the time of the final poems. Given Milton's evolving theological stance, this unorthodoxy was inevitable. If the Son were consubstantial with the Father, if he were one manifestation of a Trinitarian unity, then Milton's belief in freedom would be invalid. *Paradise Regained* would cease in large part to be meaningful, since there would be no true temptation. A Christ who is in fact the Father would not succumb to Satan's temptations; a Christ who shares divine attributes, but who is nonetheless capable of independent choice, *might*—and that is the possibility which gives Milton's brief epic its power. Christ's mediatory office demanded, in Milton's view at least, that the Son be as free to choose as was the Father. The Son, in order to be free, must be both subordinate to and separate from the Father, and this is precisely the definition which Milton accepts.

* * * * * * *

---

[65] *CPW*, VI, p. 68.

Historically, Arius was among the first to define the Son as separate entirely from the Father. Like many divisive questions which afflicted the early Church, this one was based on a conflict between Christian teachings and pagan philosophy. Since philosophy emphasized a monotheistic universe, regardless of the name by which that monad might be known, the early Christian definition of the relationship between Father and Son grew increasingly questionable. In what sense were the Father and Son—not to mention the Holy Ghost—one, and in what sense could each be considered a separate God? Athanasius taught that Jesus was in no sense subordinate to the Father and had in fact existed eternally equal to and consubstantial with the Father. Arius, on the other hand, taught that Jesus was a mere creature, created out of nothing (as was the rest of the universe), unequal with and subordinate to the Father, with a beginning (and, presumably, an end) in time. Ironically, the Bishop of Alexandria supported Athanasius's teachings on the divinity of Christ and his eternal union with the Father; and since Arius also presided over a congregation in Alexandria, the Alexandrian Church, one of the most influential of the early Christian centuries, was divided over a tenet fundamental to Christianity itself.

The split intensified as each party attempted to prove the validity of its views. Athanasius reasoned that the Word was not created, but rather begotten, and that

> To beget is to produce a perfect image of one's self, and to communicate all that is within one's self, one's substance, one's nature, one's glory; and it is thus that the Father produced the Son.[66]

As proof texts, Athanasius chose "I and my Father are one" (John 10:30), "the Father is in me and I in him" (John 10:38), and "for he that hath seen me hath seen the Father" (John 14:9). For Arius, on the other hand, God was one, eternal, not born. All other beings were creatures, and of these, the Logos was the first. Like other

---

[66] James Barker, pp. 261-262.

creatures, he was created out of nothing, rather than from divine substance. God adopted Christ as Son by His own will; but by this adoption it did not follow that Christ had any participation in Divinity or resemblance to God. As absolute God cannot have an equal.[67]

Like Athanasius, Arius looked to the Scriptures for proof; unlike his opponent, he found scriptural support from the Old *and* the New Testaments: "The Lord possessed me in the beginning of his way, before his works of old" (Proverbs 8:22); "But of that day and that hour knoweth no man, no, not the angels which are in heaven, neither the Son, but the Father" (Mark 13:32); "for my Father is greater than I" (John 14:28); "And this is life eternal, that they may know thee, and Jesus Christ, whom thou hast sent" (John 17:3); "The Son can do nothing of himself" (John 5:19); "Why callest thou me good? There is none good, but one, that is God" (Mark 10:18); and "Wherefore God also hath highly exalted him, and given him a name which is above every name" (Philippians 2:9). In addition, Arius cited passages which represented Christ as suffering, growing in wisdom, and changing.

Ultimately, the Council of Nicaea proposed a compromise which most of its representatives could accept but which effectively rendered the Arian "heresy" impossible. The Son was declared to be of one substance or essence with the Father, and to describe that relationship the term *Homoousion* was coined. The conclusions reached by the council were impossible to state in exclusively scriptural terms, and the creed established was not in complete harmony with the earlier Church Fathers, neither as to the nature of the Father nor as to His relationship with the Son. The term *Homoousion* (one substance) was not scriptural and the views of Athanasius were foreign to the beliefs of the Church Fathers of the earlier centuries. Thus the "most fundamental beliefs of the historical churches cannot be traced farther back than the Council of Nicaea (325 A. D.)."[68] Essentially, then, both Arius and Athanasius represented a departure from original orthodoxy.

---

[67] James Barker., p. 241. Much of the following historical discussion is drawn from Barker, 241-262.

[68] James Barker., pp. 266-267.

After several decades of uncertainty, with first Athanasianism and then Arianism favored, the Emperor Gratian forced acceptance of dogmatic Athanasianism on the Church. From 378, the Athanasian view was that of the Catholic Church, and like so many other points of belief in the early Church, it was determined by political, not strictly theological, necessity.

Milton's refusal to believe blindly in the dictates of Catholic conciliar decisions—particularly when those dictates ran counter to the demonstrable teachings of the Scriptures and the Apostolic Fathers—is reflected in his belief concerning the nature of Christ. If both Arius and Athanasius diverged from the teachings of the original church, it is not unexpected that Milton would hesitate to accept fully the tenets of either. Kelley notes that an early scholar, Phillipus van Limborch, recognized Milton's departure from Athanasianism. When the manuscript of *The Christian Doctrine* was sent to van Limborch for evaluation, he replied that Arian tenets were discernible throughout the treatise.[69] Lewalski also notes that Milton denies the basic beliefs of post-Nicene Catholicism. She questions whether the poet's view of the Son really separates Christ "much more radically from the rest of creation and really united him much more firmly to God than the Arian Son created from nothing," and acknowledges that even though Milton obviously rejects Athanasianism, he refuses to accept Arianism in its original form.[70]

The debates between Kelley and Patrides, however, more directly investigate Milton's beliefs. Kelley states that the terms "Arian" and "antitrinitarian" are interchangeable, even though Milton does not always strictly adhere to Arius's beliefs. Kelley points out that the words were commonly interchanged during the Renaissance, not only in English but also in Polish and Latin.[71] Consequently, Kelley sees no need to debate further whether Milton was specifically Arian or antitrinitarian; he was by definition and convention interchangeably both.

---

[69] *CPW*, VI, p. 38.
[70] Lewalski, p. 145.
[71] *CPW*, VI, p. 53n.

On the other hand, Patrides—seconded by Hunter and Adamson—denies Kelley's thesis. Patrides considers Milton a subordinationist, whose understanding of the nature of the Son differs distinctly from that of the Arians. In his review of Kelley's edition of *The Christian Doctrine*, Patrides takes Kelley severely to task for failing to discuss Milton as a subordinationist and for ignoring the arguments of Neoplatonists like Philo and Plotinus as well as Christian Fathers such as Tertullian for subordinationism, itself a major tenet of the pre-Nicene Church and thus of interest for Milton as a believer in the purity of primitive Christianity. The subordinationists argued for a sharing of substance between the Father and the Son, which Milton would in part have accepted. In addition, Milton would probably have agreed with their definition of the Son as inferior to and separate from the Father rather than one manifestation of a single being.[72]

In yet another attempt at defining the union between the Father and the Son, Curry concludes that for Milton,

> the essence of the Father cannot be communicated to another person; the Son is distinguished also in his own essence, and "since a numerical difference originates in difference in essence, those who are two numerically must be also two essentially".... The Son, therefore, cannot possibly be coessential with God the Father; he is clearly a subordinate and independent essence produced as an effect by the will of God, from whom all things proceed.[73]

The Son, as subordinate creation, shares only peripherally in the Father's metaphysical attributes and is thus in some sense mutable, fi-

---

[72] Patrides, "An Open Letter on the Yale Edition of *De Doctrina Christiana*," *MQ*, VII, 3 (October 1973), pp. 72-73. See also the series of essays on the nature of the Father and of the Son in *Bright Essence: Studies in Milton's Theology*, ed. William B. Hunter, Jr., C. A. Patrides, and J. H. Adamson (Salt Lake City, Utah: The University of Utah Press, 1971); Lewalski, pp. 141-142

[73] Curry, p. 28, also 31-32..

nite, and corruptible. Lewalski agrees with Curry at this point, suggesting that the Son possesses attributes of the Father because of a "conscious donation [by] the Father." The Son participates in Godhood only insofar as the Father extends the relevant powers and gifts to him.[74]

As varied as these critical evaluations might be, however, they do generally share two basic conclusions concerning Milton's incorporation of Arian or subordinationist heterodoxy into his conception of the Son: in Milton's theology, the Son is separate from and subordinate to the Father, yet the Son shares attributes with the Father, including perfect freedom of choice. Christ has "freedom to act creatively rather than from necessity; the Son has attained his oneness with God by choice (both his own and God's) and not by an originate identity...."[75] Milton's Christ is, as Satan acknowledges,

> With more than human gifts from Heav'n adorn'd,
> Perfections absolute, Graces divine,
> And amplitude of mind to greatest Deeds.
> (*PR*, II, 137-139)

Christ is potentially as free and unrestricted by necessity as is the Father.

Milton's emphasis on Christ's freedom of choice inevitably colors the poet's responses to Christ's mediatorial function as the Son. The sacrifice of the Son of God as an atonement for the sons of man, for instance, frequently seems less important than the ethical example of the Son, who through proper choice, defines and confirms his "begetting" as Redeemer. As in Milton's earlier poems, including "Upon the Circumcision," the passages in *Paradise Lost* which mention the Crucifixion avoid explicit references to torture and pain. The physical elements of the event are far overshadowed by the moral and spiritual. In "The Passion," which requires that Milton directly confront the Crucifixion, the poet demonstrates persistent

---

[74] Lewalski, p. 147.
[75] Diane McColley, "Free Will and Obedience in the Separation Scene of *Paradise Lost*," *SEL*, 12 (Winter 1973), p. 110.

unwillingness to deal with the necessary images. The Crucifixion is, of course, necessary to the final redemption of man, but Christ must first *choose* to redeem man and to accept without hesitation any degradation and pain in order to carry out his mission. For Milton, the Son's mental acceptance of the Crucifixion was more meaningful than its physical terrors. Louis L. Martz suggests that this concentration on the function of the Son, as opposed to a concentration on his personality, is characteristic of the seventeenth century. We hear much of Christ the Mediator and the Redeemer, but "of the man, the babe in the manger, the suffering servant on the cross, we hear remarkably little...."[76]

The Incarnation is the central Christian mystery for Milton, the choice by which Christ voluntarily undertook to provide a paradigm of proper choice for erring man. Milton's Christ mediates between God and man, between Creator and creation. Christ's hypostatic union of two natures—God's and man's—allows him to experience both levels of existence, and within each he acts with unbounded freedom. Indeed, while *Paradise* Lost emphasizes Christ as the Son, Paradise *Regained* primarily confronts the question of Christ's freedom as man. Through his gradual accretion of knowledge he arrives at a true understanding of his dual nature and of his mission and, by the end of the poem, is perfect in freedom of choice as both son of Mary and Son of God. In his dual role as God and man, the Son lends coherence and unity to the universe. Christ thus reflects the moral freedom bestowed upon him by the Father and makes essential the extension of that freedom to humanity, since it is as man that the Son will, through proper choice, effect man's regeneration.

Milton returns frequently to the theme of man's salvation and regeneration as results of the Son's freedom of choice and action. In *The Christian Doctrine*, Milton defines the importance of the Son to man: "Except for Christ, then who was foreknown, no grace was decided upon, no reconciliation between God and man who was going to fall" (I, iv, 175-176). This thesis is restated in *Paradise Lost* as:

---

[76] Louis M. Martz, *The Poetry of Meditation* (New Haven: Yale University Press, 1954), p. 2

> And now without redemption all mankind
> Must have been lost, adjudg'd to Death and Hell
> By doom severe, had not the Son of God,
> In whom the fulness dwells of love divine,
> His dearest mediation thus renew'd....
> Behold mee then, mee for him, life for life
> I offer, on mee let thine anger fall;
> Account mee man; I for his sake will leave
> Thy bosom, and this glory next to thee
> Freely put off, and for him lastly die
> Well pleas'd....
>
> (III, 222-226, 236-241)

Without the Son, redemption is impossible; and the mediatorial office of the Son requires his unimpaired freedom of choice.

ii. The Early Poems

Although Milton's conception of the Son altered considerably during his lifetime, the early poems show that Milton nonetheless consistently emphasized the absolute freedom of the Son, even when the exact nature of the relationship between the Father and the Son remained ambiguous or obscured. Thus "On the Morning of Christ's Nativity," while suggesting an orthodox, Trinitarian interpretation of the Godhead, still centers on Christ's volitive, mediatorial function.

The purpose of Milton's Nativity Ode, unlike that of such nearly contemporary nativity poems as Crashaw's "Hymn in the Holy Nativity,"[77] is to trace the process by which the Son

> ...our deadly forfeit should release

---

[77] Rosemond Tuve (*Images and Themes in Five Poems by Milton* [Cambridge, Massachusetts: Harvard University Press], 1957), Hanford, Ruth Wallerstein (*Richard Crashaw: A Study in Style and Poetic Development* [Madison, Wisconsin: University of Wisconsin Press], 1959), and Martz (*Poetry of Meditation*) all discuss the Nativity poems in terms of an opposition between counter-Reformation and Protestant.

> And with his Father work us a perpetual peace.
>
> (6-7)

The poem's concern with Christ as essential to human redemption reflects Milton's decision to attempt something traditional but not quite conventional in his treatment of the Incarnation.[78] This suggestion of unconventionality is further supported by the organization of the poem; the reader is greeted, not with the anticipated manger, shepherds, and angel choruses as in Crashaw's poem, but rather with a reference to Christ's

> ...glorious Form, that Light unsufferable,
> And that far-beaming blaze of Majesty,
> Wherewith he wont at Heav'n's high Council-Table,
> To sit the midst of Trinal Unity,
> He laid aside; and here with us to be,
> Forsook the Courts of everlasting Day,
> And chose with us a darksome House of mortal Clay.
>
> (8-14)

This is not the Babe of Crashaw's counter-Reformation ritual love poem, comfortable in his "balmy nest," but rather the divine Son of an ineffable God, a warrior endowed with strength and freedom, who voluntarily assumed mortality and death, the only mode by which to raise man to immortality and life. The decision of the Son, represented by the well-placed verb *chose*, is virtually that of the Celestial Council of *Paradise Lost* (III), in which the Son takes upon himself the commitment to Incarnation.

Throughout the Nativity Ode we never forget the God of might and majesty whom Milton delineates in the opening lines. Within the first stanza of the hymn proper, the Son moves quickly from

> ...the Heav'n-born child,
> All meanly wrapped in the rude manger...

---

[78] Tuve, p. 40; Marilyn Arnold, "Milton's Accessible God: The Role of the Son in *Paradise Lost*," *MQ*, VII, 3 (October 1973), p. 69.

(30-31)

to the Master-Creator of the world:

> Nature in awe to him
> Hath doff'd her gaudy trim,
>   With her great Master so to sympathize....
>
> (32-34)

In this "severely Protestant" hymn, we join the poet in examining the means by which redemption is made available: the re-establishment of universal harmony of the spheres; the return of the Golden Age at the command of the Prince of Light; the final judgment of the world by the "dreadful Judge of Middle Air"; and the silencing of the pagan oracles by the infant.

Only at the end of the poem, after a stanza which in Crashaw would have been intensely sensual but which in Milton's work punctuates the utter defeat of the demons—only then will Milton draw the reader explicitly to the manger and the child. Even here, however, the impact is of power and might, not of softness and love:

> Time is our tedious Song should here have ending;
> Heav'n's youngest-teemed Star
> Hath fixt her polisht Car,
>   Her sleeping Lord with Handmaid Lamp attending:
> And all about the Courtly Stable,
> Bright-harness'd Angels sit in order serviceable.
>
> (239-244)

Even as sleeping infant, Milton's Son of God lies surrounded with the glory of his godhead and the power of his freedom.

Much has been said concerning imagery and theme in the Nativity Ode, demonstrating that the poem is intensely Protestant in its treatment of the Son and that it concentrates on attributes unusual in a Nativity poem; but such elements ultimately relate to Milton's conception of the Son as free agent and of the Son's decision to provide redemption for humankind. For Milton, the physical Incarnation was less important than Christ's decision; hence his Christmas poem largely ignores the tender Babe in order to delineate the process by which Christ's choice affects humanity.

The Nativity Ode, "The Passion," and "Upon the Circumcision" are frequently read as a trilogy dealing with critical episodes in the Son's mortality. As a result, readers justly anticipate that the latter poems will also emphasize Christ's freedom as mediator. In the Nativity Ode, the poet as *persona* appears briefly in the introductory stanzas, but effectively disappears as the Hymn proceeds. Throughout "The Passion," on the other hand, Milton is conscious of himself as poet writing a poem; he seems less able than before to submerge himself. By stanza V, for example, the persona of the speaker has interfered with the ostensible subject of the Son's passion, with a resulting concentration on the internal grief of the poet rather than on the external suffering of the Son, leading to the final lines,

> And I (for grief is easily beguil'd)
>   Might think th'infection of my sorrows loud
> Had got a race of mourners on some pregnant cloud.
> (54-56)

The poem is inwardly directed, self-oriented, and profoundly personal. The poet apparently finds it impossible to imagine the suffering of the Son in any other way than by analyzing the impact of that suffering—and concomitantly of the Son's *decision* to suffer—on himself. The poem becomes a vehicle for the poet's own grief in contemplating the Crucifixion.

Again, this quality in the poem relates to Milton's conception of the Son. For Milton, the actual death of Christ—though ever-present in his theology—pales in importance when compared with the Son's declaration of his willingness to put the process of redemption irrevocably in motion. In "The Passion," merely two stanzas are devoted to the Son and in those the authorial *I* occurs infrequently. Significantly, both stanzas refer only indirectly to the actual Passion and Crucifixion. In stanza II, the author speaks in the beginning lines:

> For now to sorrow must I tune my song,

> And set my Harp to notes of saddest woe,
>
> (8-9)

and not until stanza IV does he again intrude. In every other stanza, however, the authorial *I*, *me*, and *my* literally force the reader away from contemplating the Passion to contemplating the poet. In addition, only the second and third stanzas refer directly to the choice which preordained the Passion. As Milton alludes to Hercules—and thereby to the Renaissance tradition of the choice of Hercules[79]—and to the Son's assumption of the burden of redemption, he defines the importance of the Passion:

> Dangers, and snares, and wrongs, and worse than so,
> Which he for us did freely undergo:
>   Most perfect *Hero*, tried in heaviest plight
> Of labors huge and hard, too hard for human wight.
>
> (11-14)

The difficult, heroic labors are not merely physical suffering and pain; these are contributory but not of the first order. The more intense suffering preceded the Passion.

    The subsequent stanza traces the progress of the Son:

> He sovereign Priest, stooping his regal head
> That dropt with odorous oil down his fair eyes,
> Poor fleshly Tabernacle entered,
> His starry front low-rooft beneath the skies;
> O what a Mask was there, what a disguise!
>   Yet more; the stroke of death he must abide,
> Then lies him meekly down fast by his Brethren's side.
>
> (15-21)

---

[79] See Erwin Panofsky, *Hercules am Scheideweg und andere antike Bildstoffe in der neueren Kunst* (Leipzig: B. G. Teubner, 1930); for a discussion of the Hercules motif, see also Seaman, p. 31.

In order to emphasize the actions preceding them, the Passion, Crucifixion, and Death of Christ are cursorily dismissed in one line; nowhere else in the poem are they mentioned. The Son suffered when he initially committed himself to redeeming humanity, fully realizing the physical and mental pains he would endure. Milton could respond to Christ as "Sovereign Priest," damp with the oil of consecration, or as immortal assuming mortality to reconcile God and man. His ingrained respect for perfect freedom of choice perfectly exercised determined the form, content, and ultimately the failure of "The Passion." Unable to approach a subject which disallowed his wonted emphasis on the absolute freedom of the Son's offer and mission, the poet drifted from the Passion, to himself as poet struggling to find importance in the physical manifestation of a decision long-before reached, and finally into silence.

In "Upon the Circumcision," although the poem still moves more inwardly than outwardly, the *I* so prevalent in "The Passion" has been replaced by the more general *we*. The quasi-epic invocation and incremental periodic structure of the opening lines,

> Ye flaming Powers, and winged Warriors bright,
> That erst with Music and triumphant song
> First heard by happy watchful Shepherds' ear,
> So sweetly sung your Joy the Clouds along
> Through the soft silences of the list'ning night,
> Now mourn...,
>
> (1-6)

recapitulates in miniature Milton's evocation of power and might in the Nativity Ode. As in "The Passion," the pain and agony associated with the Circumcision relate not merely to the Heavenly Babe but also to the poet and his audience:

> ...if sad share with *us* to bear
> Your fiery essence can distill no tear,
> Burn in your sighs, and borrow
> Seas wept from *our* deep sorrows....
>
> (6-9; italics mine)

The Circumcision poem forms part of a larger unit by focusing upon Christ's sacrifice and by looking from that act to more extended meanings. Within the twenty-eight lines of the poem, the reader is directed from the Circumcision backward to the Incarnation and forward to the Passion and the Crucifixion.

These three essential episodes of Christ's redemptive mission are simultaneously present in the single occasion of the Circumcision. The beginning of Christ's mortality requires his forsaking the glories of Heaven and putting on the human; the beginning of his mediation entails the shedding of blood in the Circumcision. His life begins, as it will end, with a passion, yet the central passages of the poem deal not with the infant's pain, nor with the greater sorrows to come, nor with the moment of Incarnation; they are instead concerned with the application of these three great episodes to the process of human-kind's redemption and renovation:

> O more exceeding love or law more just?
> Just law indeed, but more exceeding love!
> For we by rightful doom remediless
> Were lost in death, till he that dwelt above
> High-thron'd in secret bliss, for us frail dust
> Emptied his glory, ev'n to nakedness....
>
> (15-20)

This is the message of the poem, redemption made possible by Christ's decision "before the foundation of the world," now made efficacious through the triple sacrifice symbolically present in the Circumcision. The Atonement is given immediacy through the present reference, "And that great Cov'nant which we still transgress" (1. 21); the freedom of man to choose evil over good makes essential the Son's choice to reverse that perversion of freedom and provide a paradigm of proper choice. The might and majesty of the infant Christ, which in the Nativity Ode was sufficient to silence the pagan oracles, is here revealed in the ritual of Circumcision, which "seals obedience first with wounding smart/This day...." Christ's choice is to obey the law which he comes to fulfill for the sake of men.

iii. The Epics

The culmination of Milton's presentations of the Son is found in *Paradise Lost* and *Paradise Regained*, in which the Son appears not merely as subject but also as character. One of the frequent questions asked about the epics, particularly *Paradise Lost*, is: "If the poems belong to the heroic tradition, who then are their heroes?" Critics have varied in their responses. Several of the Romantics claimed that Milton had unconsciously intended the Satan of Books I and II as hero, then willfully degraded him after becoming aware of the grandeur with which he was portraying the Father of Lies. Others have considered Adam and Eve as the only possible heroic figures, since, to use Northrop Frye's classification, divine beings belong to myth, not to epic.[80] Yet others have suggested that heroic virtue can only be couched in the figure of Christ, the only viable heroic-epic character in either *Paradise Lost* or *Paradise Regained*. Satan, the archetype of Christian anti-heroism, who represents the traditional Achillean martial hero of classical tradition (itself a paradigm of false choice), is immediately disqualified, while Adam is a model of heroic potential which fails. But above them both the figure of the Son embodies a more inclusive, more complete, and for Milton more truthful model of Christian heroism, in all of the ambiguities implicit in the term, encompassing all lesser sorts.

Regardless of any precise definition of *heroic* and *hero* in *Paradise Lost*, however, the Son is one of two exempla of true, unfallen *choice*, Abdiel being the second. Through Christ, and to a lesser degree through Abdiel, Milton constructs a model of the freedom essential to man's regeneration. Christ's offer of sacrifice is given both freely and—simultaneously and paradoxically—in strict obedience to the will of the Father. By voluntarily submitting his will to that of the Father, the Son receives that broader freedom which, accompa-

---

[80] Northrop Frye, *Anatomy of Criticism* (New York: Atheneum, 1967), pp. 33-34.

nying true obedience, is denied to those who choose license and enslaving selfishness. Through the Son's decision to act in perfect harmony with the Father's will, he provides the only possible link among all levels of the universe, uniting God with the angels and humanity. The Son is King in Heaven through his exaltation by the Father and King on earth through his mediatorial function, to bring about the reconciliation of fallen humanity with God.

Milton's purpose in Book III of *Paradise Lost* is in part to define Christ's selflessness in voluntarily accepting a dual role as God and man. Before doing so, however, Milton carefully defines false, selfish choice—epitomized by Satan and his Infernal Council—in order that the reader might appreciate the righteousness of Christ's choices. In Books I and II, Milton presents Satan, the fallen angels, Hell, and Pandemonium, and invites participation in a demonic council in which all of the appearances of unhampered choice among equals are carefully preserved, superficially at least. Having been defeated by the "Thunderer," Satan scrupulously avoids the overt semblance of tyrannical hegemony over his fellows, although he ultimately aims for absolute control, for an oriental despotism—suggested imagistically by references to *Babylon* and *Alcairo*—modeled perversely on the just monarchy of Heaven. By allowing the hollow *forms* of choice to the fallen angels, Satan consolidates his control over them and enslaves them further to that will which has already lost them the joys of Heaven. And, lest others subsequently volunteer to accompany him and share unearned his glory, Satan, now "The Monarch," summarily dissolves the council. While Satan undertakes the destruction of man, the demons are allowed only to explore Hell, devise equally hollow epic games, or sit and—ironically, from the reader's perspective—speculate

> In thoughts more elevate, and [reason] high
> Of Providence, Foreknowledge, Will, and Fate,
> Fixt Fate, Free will, Foreknowledge absolute,
> And [find] no end, in wand'ring mazes lost.
> <div align="right">(<i>PL</i>, II, 558-561)</div>

As Satan begins his journey to earth, Milton takes us directly to Heaven for a second council. If, because of their confidence in reason unaided by faith, the demons are unable to find their way through the "mazes" of philosophical speculation, the angels in Book III are fully instructed in Providence, Foreknowledge, Free Will, and Fate by the Father Himself; and in addition, Christ is introduced as a personification of absolute freedom. By contrast with Satan and the fallen angels, Christ exposes Hell's much-vaunted freedom as absolute bondage to self and sin. Paradoxically, the Council in Heaven displays no such alternative plans as had the demonic council. The Father perceives Adam and Eve on earth and Satan winging through the Gulf. He foreknows perfectly the fall:

> For Man will heark'n to his glozing lies,
> And easily transgress the sole Command,
> Sole pledge of his obedience: So will fall
> Hee and his faithless Progeny....
> *(PL,* III, 93-96)

With that fall (freely entered into, although man was in part deceived) comes the irrevocable decree of death:

> He with his whole posterity must die,
> Die hee or Justice must; unless for him
> Some other able, and as willing, pay
> The rigid satisfaction, death for death.
> *(PL,* III, 203-212)

Here is no toying with alternative plans, with discussions from lesser councilors. The Father is aware both of the inherent freedom in man which will result in his fall and of His own restrictions. To act other than as decreed would be to contravene His own nature and thus enter into a contradiction, the one capability which Milton denies his God.

At the question "Dwells in all Heaven charity so dear?" the divine concourse stands mute, just as the demons in Pandemonium had done at Satan's arrogation of power unto himself, until the Son speaks and offers himself as ransom. Through inversely parallel epic councils, Milton unmistakably contrasts Satan, seeking greater glory for himself at the expense of innocent man, with the Son, seeking greater glory for the Father through depriving himself on behalf of humankind. After making his offer, Christ encounters a silence superficially similar to that which Satan used so dramatically to further his selfish plans. Yet in Heaven, the angels are truly capable of choice, and when the decision is reached, they are allowed to respond. The Son's offer is free from posturing, grandiloquent maneuverings, or Machiavellian plotting. There is instead the renunciation of Godhood to assume mortality and death in order that mercy and justice may be united. Christ has no more foreknowledge of the final events than has Satan, but he does enjoy one advantage over his infernal adversary—the Son acts through faith and obedience freely embraced.

In Book III, then, Milton defines the Son in part by contrast with Hell and in part by the actions of the Father, the Son, and the angels. The Son accepts responsibility for fallen and doomed humanity through his complete faith in and obedience to the will of the Father. His offer of mediation, entered into willingly, corresponds to both the freedom which the Father perfectly demonstrates and the freedom of man which will allow the Fall to occur. The illusion of freedom in the Infernal Council results in increasingly onerous bondage for Satan, the devils, and those who choose to follow them; the apparent autocracy of Heaven, which is in fact a manifestation of perfect liberty, results in the voluntary mediation of the Son and the possibility of future redemption for the faithful among Adam's progeny.

Milton allows an apparent contradiction between the Son's dependence upon and obedience to the Father in Book III, and his apparent martial prowess later in the poem, when he appears on the scene of battle accompanied by all the panoply of a Homeric hero. Even so, the second major appearance of the Son underscores the conclusions reached during the Celestial Council. The Son states openly that

> O Father, O Supreme of Heav'nly Thrones,

> First, Highest, Holiest, Best, thou always seek'st
> To glorify thy Son, I always thee,
> As is most just; this I my Glory account,
> My exaltation, and my whole delight,
> That thou in me well pleas'd, declar'st thy will
> Fulfill'd, which to fulfil is all my bliss.
> Sceptre and Power, thy giving, I assume,
> And gladlier shall resign, when in the end
> Thou shalt be All in All, and I in thee
> For ever, and in mee all whom thou lov'st....
> 				(*PL*, VI, 723-733)

This is the Son as he appears throughout *Paradise Lost*: the perfect image of perfect freedom, acting within the boundaries of obedience and love, having as his only goals the glorification of God and the fulfillment of the Father's desires.

* * * * * * *

As might be expected, *Paradise Regained* provides more substantial insight into the character of Christ than does *Paradise Lost*. In the earlier epic, Milton confronts man's fall through improper exercise of will, with the Son functioning primarily as a contrast and exemplar of proper will; in *Paradise Regained*, Milton sings

> Recover'd Paradise to all mankind,
> By one man's firm obedience fully tried
> Through all temptation, and the Tempter foil'd
> In all his wiles, defeated and repuls't,
> And Eden rais'd in the waste Wilderness.
> 				(*PR*, I, 3-7)

In *Paradise Regained*, the emphasis has shifted from the external choices made by the first man and woman to the internal decisions of the Christ. His responses to the various temptations are, in fact, less essential than the motivation for those responses. For example, he refuses the feast proffered by Satan, not because feasting is immoral, but because of the devotedly evil source of the banquet, as is shown when he later accepts viands offered by angels. Throughout the poem, Milton continually restates his concern for the power of an internal freedom which can be developed fully only by the Son. In Book II, this freedom is defined:

> Yet he who reigns within himself, and rules
> Passions, Desires, and Fears, is more a King;
> Which every wise and virtuous man attains:
> And who attains not, ill aspires to rule
> Cities of men, or headstrong Multitudes,
> Subject himself to Anarchy within,
> Or lawless passions in him, which he serves.
>
> (*PR*, II, 466-472)

Although Christ refers in these lines to the functions of earthly magistrates, his speech also reflects his conceptions of his divine role. He must, as perfect man and Son of God, meet in every detail the requirements of internal control, and Milton indicates in other portions of the poem that this is exactly what Christ has accomplished.

In the Divine Councils of both *Paradise Lost* and *Paradise Regained*, the Father clearly defines the sources of Christ's status as the Son. The first is his generation by the Father; the second is his elevation, the metaphorical "begetting" of *Paradise Lost*, which in *Paradise Regained* is indicated by the birth of Christ through the power of the Holy Ghost (I, 140-143). Finally, Christ's superiority to Satan had been irrevocably determined in *Paradise Lost* as the Son was recognized by the Father:

> Hear my Decree, which unrevok't shall stand.
> This day I have begot whom I declare
> My only Son, and on this holy Hill
> Him have anointed, whom ye now behold
> At my right hand; your Head I him appoint;
> And by my Self have sworn to him shall bow
> All knees in Heav'n, and shall confess him Lord....
>
> (*PL*, V, 600-606)

Thus the authority of Christ, as he appears in the epics, rests upon three fundamental attributes: his generation as the Son; his endowment by the Father with the rights and powers of Godhood; and through his birth into mortality, his unique stature as Son of God and son of man.

There is an additional factor, however, in the elevation of Christ—the decision of Christ to obey the will of the Father. In the Council in Book III of *Paradise Lost*, the Father had outlined for the Son the consequences of the latter's choices to assume mortality and to satisfy the demands of justice through extending mercy to man. Among other things the Son was told,

> Nor shalt thou by descending to assume
> Man's Nature, lessen or degrade thine own.
> Because thou hast, though Thron'd in highest bliss
> Equal to God, and equally enjoying
> God-like fruition, quitted all to save
> A world from utter loss, and hast been found
> By Merit more than Birthright Son of God,
> Found worthiest to be so by being Good,
> Far more than Great or High; because in thee
> Love hath abounded more than Glory abounds....
> (*PL*, III, 303-312)

The unique position of the Son therefore owes as much to his conscious acceptance of the responsibilities and requirements of his mission as to his elevation by divine decree. The Son is so elevated because the Father, in His omniscience, foresees the choices that Christ will make. The Father knows the Son and places implicit trust in him, allowing Satanic temptations in order to define the divine powers and attributes of the Only Begotten. Christ cannot fail, not because of the intervention of the Father, but because of his awareness of his own internal strengths, faith, and freedom. The Son's decision to remain true to his responsibilities results in what Satan rightly recognizes as divine powers:

> If he be Man by Mother's side at least
> With more than human gifts from Heav'n adorn'd,
> Perfections absolute, Graces divine,
> And amplitude of mind to greatest Deeds.
> *(PR,* II, 136-139)

Through exercising proper choice, Christ reasserts his birthright as the Son and, as a result, is sustained and guided in his functions by the all-encompassing powers of the Father.

In *Paradise Regained,* the reader observes not only Christ's responses to temptations as both God and man, but also his creation of a model of obedience for erring man. In contrast to Adam and Eve, who succumbed to the temptation to achieve quickly what Raphael suggested they might attain when man had at last turned "all to spirit,/Improv'd by tract of time" *(P.L.,* V, 497-498), Christ repudiates the insidious suggestion that he might establish his kingdom on earth sooner than God intended. Satan urges:

> If Kingdom move thee not, let move thee Zeal
> And Duty; Zeal and Duty are not slow,
> But on Occasion's forelock watchful wait.
> They themselves rather are occasion best,
> Zeal of thy Father's house, Duty to free
> Thy Country from her Heathen servitude;
> So shalt thou best fullfil, best verify
> The Prophets old, who sung thy endless reign,
> The happier reign the sooner it begins.
> Reign then; what canst thou better do the while?
> *(PR,* III, 171-180)

To which temptation Christ, recognizing the subtle exchange of divine Foreknowledge for mere chance and fortune, immediately replies:

> All things are best fulfill'd in their due time,
> And time there is for all things, Truth hath said:
> If of my reign Prophetic Writ hath told

> That it shall never end, so when begin
> The Father in his purpose hath decreed,
> He in whose hand all times and seasons roll.
>
> (*PR*, III, 182-187)

Christ recognizes that by acting on his own initiative he will, instead of freeing Israel from her "Heathen servitude," merely replace one bondage with a tyranny of self-imprisonment. He knows that he can restore freedom to humankind and establish the Father's Kingdom only by limiting his actions to suit the Father's will. Were he to respond to Satan's urging or to his own willful desires, he would be limiting himself through the exercise of license unlimited. Part of understanding his divine mission must be to realize that "of the day and hour knoweth no man, no, not the angels which are in heaven, neither the Son, but the Father" (Mark 13:32). The scripture does not, of course, refer directly to the events of the temptation, particularly as Milton expands upon them. It does, however, provide warrant for the Son's refusal to accept Satan's challenge. The Son recognizes that he must await the Father's will to announce his Godhead.

The Father knows that the Son will not fail this test. He has foreseen that Christ will repair the wound inflicted by Adam's and Eve's precipitous actions and will effect a reconciliation between Heaven and earth. Early in *Paradise Regained*, the angels sing:

> The Father knows the Son; therefore secure
> Ventures his filial Virtue, though untried,
> Against whate'er may tempt, whate'er seduce,
> Allure, or terrify, or undermine.
> Be frustrate, all ye stratagems of Hell,
> And devilish machinations come to nought.
>
> (*PR*, I, 176-181)

For the test to be truly effective, however, the Son cannot foreknow absolutely the outcome. If the Son were fully aware of his divinity, there could be no conflict; Satan would simply be an unseeing fool, and the Son would be cruelly toying with an unworthy adversary. For temptations to be functional, the Son must be capable of growth, of volition, and ultimately of failure.

In order to evaluate the role of the Son in the poem, one must remember the importance Milton places on the freedom of choice particularly essential to Christ's mediatorial office. For humanity to achieve restoration, the Son must make true choices and depend wholly upon faith and obedience, rather than upon the foreknowledge of the Father. When the Son is alone and unchallenged, his divinity becomes less essential and he seems more human. When confronted by Satan, Christ confirms his "begetting." Each successive temptation strengthens his consciousness of the hypostatic union of two natures within him.

Christ is described from varying points of view throughout the epic: the Father's, Satan's, the narrator's, and his own. His temptation is, in part, to determine which of those views is true and complete, and to act according to it. Through the process of the temptations, he discovers Satan's identity and consequent limitations:

> The Kingdoms of the world to thee were giv'n,
> Permitted rather, and by thee usurp't,
> Other donation none thou canst produce;
> If given, by whom but by the King of Kings,
> God over all supreme?
>
> (*PR*, IV, 182-186)

More importantly, however, the Son becomes aware of himself as Redeemer and Son of God. In the final temptation, he simultaneously declares himself God and submits himself to the desires of the Father. Satan places Christ on the pinnacle of the temple, then challenges him:

> There stand, if thou wilt stand: to stand upright
> Will ask thee skill; I to thy Father's house
> Have brought thee, and highest plac't, highest is best,
> Now show thy Progeny; if not to stand,
> Cast thyself down; safely if Son of God:
> For it is written, He will give command

> Concerning thee to his Angels, in thir hands
> They shall up lift thee, lest at any time
> Thou chance to dash thy foot against a stone.
> To whom thus Jesus. Also it is written"
> Tempt not the Lord thy God; he said and stood.
>
> (*PR*, IV, 551-561)

Satan's challenge is subtle and complex. In addition to the implied doubt in Christ's identity as Son—the thrice-repeated *if*—there is also the double-edged temptation itself. The Son may either cast himself from the pinnacle, which would suggest compliance to Satan's doubt and a testing of the Father's commandments; or stand and repeat Satan's self-damnatory arrogation of height and merit. Limited in his perceptions by his choices, Satan can perceive only an either/or response by Christ—either to stand or to cast himself down—both of which would appear to lead the Son into temptation. Christ is fully aware of his role, however. Through the four books of the epic he has grown in strength, faith, and obedience, until he can easily withstand the overt challenge—to cast himself down—by citing the Scripture which simultaneously declares his relationship with the Father. And by doing so he confirms his elevation "before the foundations of the world" to the mediatorial and redemptive office. He alone is truly worthy of standing "highest plac't." Satan's license has resulted in an apparent choice, either half of which seems damnatory. Christ's apparent limitations lead him to perfect freedom through his final assertion of Godhood.

With the second, more critical fall of Satan, the temptation and testing of the Son is completed, the "Paradise within" secured. Having made the decision in the Celestial Council of *Paradise Lost* to accomplish the redemption of humankind, and having proven true as man to that decision, Christ has made certain the subsequent events of his mission: the Passion, the Crucifixion, the Resurrection, and the reconciliation of man with God. He submits to the ministrations of angels before

> he unobserv'd
> Home to his Mother's house private return'd.

(*PR*, IV, 638-639)

As we as readers re-enter the world with Christ, we are invited to participate in his decisions, the same decisions which we all must encounter in one form or another. As the exemplar of proper choice, Christ mediates between the absolute perfection of the Father and the fallen state of man. Participating in both, he alone is capable of ultimately reuniting them; *Paradise Lost* and *Paradise Regained* delineate the processes and choices by which Christ accomplishes his mission as son of man and Son of God.

CHAPTER FIVE

The First Levels of Creation—
The Material Universe and the Angels

> When matter or form has gone out from God and become the property of another, what is there to prevent its being infected and polluted, since it is now in a mutable state, by the calculations of the devil or of man, calculations which proceed from these creatures themselves?
>
> —*The Christian Doctrine*, I, vi

i. The Material Universe

Early in his poetic career, Milton evinced a strong interest in the universe and its relationship to God and man. In an academic exercise, *Naturam non Pati Senium* (1628), Milton's views paralleled those taken the previous year in George Hakewill's *An Apologie or Declaration of the Power and Providence of God*, by arguing that the universe was not subject to decay. After recapitulating the evidence for a general decay in nature, Milton responds:

> But by founding the stars more strongly the omnipotent Father has taken thought for the Universe. He has fixed the scales of fate with sure balance and commanded every individual thing in the cosmos to hold to its course forever.

> Thus, in a word, the righteous sequence of all things shall go on perpetually, until the final fire shall destroy the world, enveloping the poles and summits of vast heaven, while the fabric of the universe consumes in a mighty funeral pyre. (Hughes, *Complete Poems*, 34-35)

Later, Milton will expand this vision of the final dissolution of the earth into a higher level of existence:

> Day and Night,
> Seed-time and Harvest, Heat and hoary Frost
> Shall hold thir course, till fire purge all things new,
> Both Heav'n and Earth, wherein the just shall dwell.
> *Paradise Lost*, XI, 898-901

In arguing against a decay in nature, Milton simultaneously emphasizes the Father's control over the universe. Indeed, the genesis, government, purpose, and final destiny of the universe are inextricably intertwined with Milton's conception of the Godhead and of the importance of freedom of choice among all rational creatures. Consequently, Milton endowed his universe with overtones both unusual and essential to his poetic purposes.

Milton states in *The Christian Doctrine* that the Father is free from any hint of external necessity and that the creation of the material universe represents the second manifestation of His absolute will. The introduction to the chapter "Of the Creation" notes:

> The second kind of external efficiency is commonly called CREATION....CREATION is the act by which GOD THE FATHER PRODUCED EVERYTHING THAT EXISTS BY HIS WORD AND SPIRIT, that is, BY HIS WILL, IN ORDER TO SHOW THE GLORY OF HIS POWER AND GOODNESS.
> (*CD*, VI, 299-300)

According to traditional theology, God's external efficiency was manifested first in the Creation and second in the Providence by which He governs that Creation. Milton places the generation of the Son as the first instance of external efficiency, however, followed by the Creation and providence.[81] Milton's definition of the generation of the Son as the first external efficiency of the Father underscores his antitrinitarianism; since the Son is generated by the Father, he shares in the substance of the Father only, not in the essence. As the first external efficiency, the Son is separate from the Father, but endowed with freedom of action and choice.

In addition, Milton's view of creation argues that the creative act, willed by the Father and accomplished by the Son (the Word) and the Divine Power (the Spirit), was a free decision which manifested the Glory, Power, and Goodness of the Father. It was a free act whereby God created all that is not God. The freedom demonstrated in the Father's generation of the Son is reflected in the creation of the material from which the visible and invisible universe is organized through the secondary efficiency of the Son. The Son quite understandably enjoys absolute freedom of choice, both as God and as man; Christ is, after all, considered throughout Milton's poetry and prose as a member of the Godhead, regardless of his subordination to the Father, and he participates in the attributes, powers, and capabilities of the Father. Yet in Milton's theology, material creations likewise participate in and enjoy the same freedom as the Son. Just as the Son's freedom is irrevocably bestowed upon him by virtue of his divine "begetting," so that same freedom is bestowed upon lower rational creatures by virtue of their relationship with the Father, contingent upon the righteousness of their choices. Milton strictly denied the orthodox *ex nihilo* interpretation of creation, according to which the Father—through divine will, power, and might, without recourse to pre-existing matter—brought into being the elements of the universe. According to proponents of *ex nihilo* creation, there was nothing except God before the creation.

Milton argued, however, that the original Hebrew, Greek, and Latin terms associated in the Scriptures with creation were best to be

---

[81] Kelley, *CPW*, VI, p. 299n.

translated as "to make out of something" (*CD*, I, vii, 305-306). As he had in interpreting the Scripture relating to the Father and the Son, Milton here rejects traditional exegesis to develop a theory of creation which more accurately accounted for the facts as he saw them. The resultant theory of creation *de deo* is an extension of Milton's concern with freedom of choice, as well as one of his unique contributions to theological speculation.[82]

Milton's reasoning is quite simple:

> It is clear, then, that the world was made out of some sort of matter. For since "action" and "passivity" are relative terms, and since no agent can act externally unless there is something, and something material, which can be acted upon, it is apparent that God could not have created this world out of nothing.
>
> (*CD*, I, vii, 307)

Milton's overt restriction on the omnipotence of the Father—that He cannot act in contradictions—also substantiates the poet's theory of creation. Milton defines the scriptural darkness, which was generally understood as the nothingness which preceded creation, as

> far from being a mere nothing: *I am Jehovah*, etc. *I form the light and create the darkness*. If the darkness is nothing, then when God created the darkness he created nothing, that is he both created and did not create, which is a contradiction in terms.
>
> (*CD*, I, VII, 306)

If the universe were created—or perhaps better expressed, *organized*—by the Father through the efficacy of the Son from pre-existing matter, what was the source of that matter? Milton notes that there are only two alternatives. The first is that matter existed co-eternally with the Father and independently of Him. This Milton finds impossible to conceive of, since matter is a principle subordi-

---

[82] Conklin, p. 67.

nate to and dependent upon God. Milton is thus forced to embrace the second alternative; matter originated from God at some point prior to the generation of the Son and the material universe. There is but "one God, the Father, from whom all things are…" (*CD*, I, vii, 306-307)

Several critics have enlarged upon the precise details of Milton's *de deo* creation. Curry suggests that Milton's materialism, of which his creation theory is a part, stems from complex philosophical backgrounds. Origen had concluded, for example, that "all rational and spiritual natures—with the exception of the Trinity alone—must always be united to bodies." Avencebrol's conception of a "plurality of forms and matters rooted in a *materia universalis*" apparently led to Milton's

> one first matter all,
> Indu'd with various forms, various degrees
> Of substance, and in things that live, of life;
> But more refin'd, more spiritous, and pure,
> As nearer to him plac't or nearer tending ….
> (*PL*, V, 472-476) [83]

In order to account for this first matter, Denis Saurat attempted to determine its precise source, arguing that the Father, as Absolute, "has neither reason nor power to change into a less perfect state," and consequently, that Milton boldly took "a passage out of the *Zohar* and made it the very center of his metaphysics":

> …I uncircumscrib'd myself retire,
> And put not forth my goodness, which is free
> To act or not….
> (*PL*, VII, 170-172)

God withdraws His will from parts of Himself, which are thus freed from His control and become the elements of the universe. As Saurat phrases it, for Milton, "Being is freedom."[84]

---

[83] Curry, pp. 161, 164.

This is basically the line of reasoning which Robins follows in *If This Be Heresy*. The retraction of God in creation is, for Robins, consistent with Milton's beliefs. Robins suggests that both Milton and Origen argued for a creation *de deo*, although their conceptions of that creation differed substantially. Both concluded that all bodies, whether of angels or of men, are in some sense material; that, as Origen wrote, even the angels have bodies, although "of such tenuousness that the gross senses of human beings are incapable of apprehending them." Both also concluded that the Father must in some manner include material substance, however pure and rarified, since all matter proceeds originally from Him:

> Matter cannot be *ex nihilo* because God is infinite, filling all space and obviating the possibility of nothingness. For matter to have existed apart from God and to have been discovered accidentally by God is precluded by God's infinity and omniscience. Since God is totality, matter cannot even emanate from him, for there would be no place to receive it. Matter comes into existence when, at the time of creation, the freed substance of God is given form through the addition of Aristotelian qualities.[85]

Milton's statements in *The Christian Doctrine* agree that all things are of God and that the Father is characterized by totality, omnipresence, immensity, and eternity.

According to the retraction theory, all things, including such vastly different forms as men and angels, are organized from primal matter, released by retraction of the Father. The elements of the material universe become more refined as they near God, their source (*PL*, V, 469-490). Man's ability to approach the Father depends upon the malleability of the primal matter from which his body is formed *and* upon his continual and volitive purification and celes-

---

[84] Denis Saurat, *Milton: Man and Thinker* (New York: The Dial Press, 1925), p. 124.

[85] Robins, pp. 77-78.

tialization. Raphael suggests one mode by which bodies may be transformed:

> ...time may come when men
> With Angels may participate, and find
> No inconvenient Diet, nor too light Fare;
> And from these corporal nutriments perhaps
> Your bodies may at last turn all to spirit,
> Improv'd by tract of time, and wing'd ascend
> Ethereal, as wee, or may at choice
> Here or in Heav'nly Paradises dwell;
> If ye be found obedient, and retain
> Unalterably firm his love entire
> Whose progeny you are.
>
> (*PL*, V, 493-503)

The apparent digression on angelic eating in Book V of *Paradise Lost* is thus no digression but rather an opportunity for Milton to state an important qualification in his definition of man and angel. Both are of the same essence and material, differing only in degree of refinement and purity. In a subsequent passage, Raphael confirms to Adam that the angels exist under conditions of absolute freedom:

> Myself and all th' Angelic Host that stand
> In sight of God enthron'd, our happy state
> Hold, as you yours, while our obedience holds;
> On other surety none; freely we serve,
> Because we freely love, as in our will
> To love or not; in this we stand or fall.
>
> (*PL*, V, 535-540)

It is precisely on this point—the freedom of creatures—that Milton seems to disagree with Origen, who argued that rational creatures attain their positions according to their various degrees of divergence from an original state of equality and purity. The freedom to diverge is bestowed upon all rational creatures by God.[86] Milton, on the other hand (according to proponents of the retraction theory), holds that the universe is free because it is composed of matter originally set free from God's control by His withdrawal. The goodness of God ceases to control directly the material universe, leaving all rational creatures free both to act and to choose whether to draw nearer to God and refine their elemental forms, or to imbrute themselves further through false choice. When creatures choose to deny God, evil enters the universe; thus Satan is the Father of Evil, since his choices occasioned the original fall from goodness.

In *This Great Argument*, however, Kelley opposes Saurat's creation-through-retraction theory. Kelley notes that the interpretation of creation as retraction rests solely upon a single passage in *Paradise Lost*, which incidentally fails to preclude creation without retraction. Kelley also states that Saurat's theory flatly contradicts assertions made about the creation in both *Paradise Lost* and *The Christian Doctrine*. The proper interpretation of the creative act is that matter

> proceeded directly from God, undigested and unadorned; and God's first encroachment on this chaos was his creation of the invisible universe—an act whereby God put forth his goodness by giving this *materia prima* order and form. After this action, which digested only a limited part of chaos, the Father returned to his natural state of rest and this left the remainder of matter in its confused, primeval state.[87]

Kelley disagrees with Saurat and Robins; in the crucial matter of freedom in the *materia prima*, however, all three agree that in one form or another the Father withdrew His influence from the elements of the universe, either at the point of creation (as in Saurat and Robins) or thereafter (as in Kelley), leaving the newly created matter

---

[86] Robins, p. 84.

[87] Maurice Kelley, *This Great Argument* (Princeton: Princeton University Press, 1941), pp. 209-210; see also Robins, p. 93.

free and unhampered by the controlling will of the Father. Milton's conceptions of freedom, of the providence and governance of God, and of predestination include the belief that matter uninfluenced by God is free. It might also be said that there is no tenet of heterodox belief to which Milton adheres more tenaciously than to the essential freedom of material creatures resulting from that creative act. Rational creatures in Milton's universe are thus endowed with a double freedom: as creations of the Father, formed of elements freed from the Father's immediate control, they enjoy a freedom of action shared by all creatures; and as rational creatures, they enjoy the freedom of choice which the Father has decreed must be concomitant with rationality.

Milton's treatment of the material universe suggests that the various levels of creation, and indeed the Father Himself, participate in a primal matter. All levels relate to each other, and all share in some sense common qualities and attributes, differing primarily in the degree of refinement of their material forms. If freedom of action is a basic attribute of the Father as well as of the Son, it then follows that the Father's creatures similarly share unhampered freedom of action, since they share the Father's divine and free substance; and if absolute freedom of choice is an attribute of both the Father and the Son, then all rational creatures likewise participate in that freedom of choice, not only because of their material forms, but also because of the Father's decrees. The continued freedom of choice among rational creatures depends, however, upon their individual receptivity to the Father's revealed will. As they choose justly, they draw nearer to Him and are elevated; as they choose unjustly, they recapitulate the falls of Satan and his cohort, embrace sin and evil, and are imbruted.

ii. Unfallen Angels

Milton often allows his theological terminology to shift away from usual definitions. He refers to God, angels, and the human soul as spirits, for example, but his usage precludes any definition of *spirit* as wholly immaterial. Angels and human souls are material, although differing in degree of refinement—and by analogy the Father and the Son are also somehow material. When referring to spirits, and especially to the angels, Milton suggests rather unorthodox entities.

Origen discusses "incorporeal" spirit as a refined, tenuous matter:

> The term...incorporeal is disused and unknown, not only in many other writings, but also in our own scriptures;...but...it must be understood to mean that he (Christ) had not such a body as demons have, which is naturally fine (subtile), and thin as if formed of air (and for that reason is either considered or called by many incorporeal), but that He had a solid and palpable body.[88]

Origen's use of scriptural authority to deny the immateriality of Christ and thereby of angels would probably have attracted Milton, even without the additional theological or philosophical support Milton might have received from Plato, Apuleius, Plotinus, Psellus, Saint Augustine and other Church Fathers, Henry More, Ralph Cudworth, and Thomas Hobbes.[89] Milton is original, however, in concluding that angels and humankind share a bond of common substance and that through the original matter from which they were created—in addition to their freedom of choice as rational beings—they enjoy a special relationship with the Father. This is not to suggest that Milton intended a pantheistic system, however. The Father had freed the original matter from His Will; hence it is no longer strictly a part of Him, although it retains the freedom which characterizes the Father. Insofar as men and angels are rational creatures and of the original substance of God, they are doubly capable of free choice. Milton specifically insists upon this agency in *The Christian Doctrine*:

---

[88] Curry, p. 161.
[89] Curry, p. 160.

The matter or object of the divine plan was that angels and men alike should be endowed with free will, so that they could either fall or not fall....

By virtue of his wisdom God decreed the creation of angels and men as beings gifted with reason and thus with free will. At the same time he foresaw the direction in which they would tend when they used this absolutely unimpaired freedom.
(*CD*, I, iii, pp. 163, 164)

Their "absolutely unimpaired freedom" remains unimpaired, however, only so long as they choose properly. As the freedom of the loyal angels and the self-imposed bondage of the rebels clearly illustrate, improper choice enslaves, binds, and limits alternatives as the chooser consciously moves farther and farther from the will of God. Consequently, the responses of the angels celestial as well as infernal to the freedom with which they are created serve as patterns upon which humans—initially less refined, more grossly corporeal than the angels—may model their actions.

The angels are free to make decisions and to take personal initiative, to follow Satan if they so desire. During the War in Heaven, they demonstrate their ability to apply their individual judgment to situations:

> ...led in fight, yet Leader seem'd
> Each Warrior single as in Chief, expert
> When to advance, or stand, or turn the sway
> Of Battle, open when, and when to close
> The ridges of grim War; no thought of flight,
> None of retreat, no unbecoming deed
> That argu'd fear; each on himself reli'd,
> As only in his arm the moment lay
> Of victory....
(*PL*, VI, 232-239)

In Milton's version of the War in Heaven, the participating angels enjoy multiple opportunities for independent and righteous choice; the loyal stand and the rebellious fall through their individual volition.

A conscious act of guile by an envious Archangel initiates the fall of the rebel angels. During the night following the convocation in which the "begetting" of the Son is announced, Satan urges his fellows to flee with him to the North, ostensibly to prepare

> Fit entertainment to receive our King
> The great *Messiah*, and his new commands,
> Who speedily through all the Hierarchies
> Intends to pass triumphant, and give Laws.
> (*PL*, V, 690-693)

Since the Heavenly Night invites sleep for all save those who sing before the unsleeping Father (V, 650-657), Satan's unwonted nocturnal activity is out of place, but it is sufficiently acceptable to beguile the one third of the Hosts who follow him to the North. There Satan erects his pavilion, blatantly called "The Palace of great *Lucifer*," a counterfeit of the Mount of the Congregation whereon the Messiah had been exalted.

From his falsely assumed height, Satan warns his followers against the dangers to their dignities and titles of

>   prostration vile,
> Too much to one, but double how endur'd,
> To one and to his image now proclaim'd?
> (*PL*, V, 782-784)

In this, his first public declaration of revolt, Satan argues partial truths in order to deceive and lead astray:

>   ye know yourselves
> Natives and Sons of Heav'n possest before
> By none, and if not equal all, yet free,
> Equally free; for Orders and Degrees

> Jar not with liberty, but well consist.
> Who can in reason then or right assume
> Monarchy over such as live by right
> His equals, if in power and splendor less,
> In freedom equal?
>
> (*PL*, V, 789-797)

Satan is guilty of two faults: first, he fails to accept the inherent superiority of the Creator-Son over creatures and instead argues for a degree of difference only, not of kind, between the newly declared Son and himself; and second, he is himself guilty of precisely the crime with which he indicts the Son. His sole purpose is the arrogation to himself of tyrannical powers over those equal to him in kind; and as they acquiesce to his falsehoods and reject the true freedom of obedience to God's righteous will, they relinquish their ability to make alternative choices and place themselves and their futures under Satan's control.

Only one angel dares to withstand Satan and draw attention to himself—Abdiel. Through Abdiel, Milton disproves the pretensions of the rebels and provides a model for repentance and for restoration to true freedom. From the beginning, the contest between the two seems unequal. Satan is superior in rank to Abdiel. He is an Archangel, "great in Power,/In favor and preeminence..." (*PL*, V, 660-661), yet he is of the same essence as Abdiel and thus has no just claim to monarchical authority over the lesser angel. Satan is capable of persuasive arguments, since through the force of his reasoning one third of the angels had enrolled in his rebellion. He is surrounded by warriors and addresses the recalcitrant Abdiel from the majesty and height of his own imitative celestial Throne.

Abdiel does not try to counter the swaying rhetoric of Satan's accusations against the Deity, however. He replies instead with what he knows to be true. God is determinedly good and, far from aspiring to demean the angels, He has as His goal their ultimate happiness:

> Yet by experience taught we know how good,
> And of our good, and of our dignity

> How provident he is, how far from thought
> To make us less, bent rather to exalt
> Our happy state under one Head more near
> United.
>
> (PL, V, 826-831)

And even granting for the moment that it is unjust that equal reign over equal, Abdiel points out, the angels are not equal in kind or degree with the "great Messiah" and thus owe obedience and honor to their Creator.

Milton has consciously placed a free agent in a situation in which a choice becomes necessary. Satan is, as Milton clearly establishes, to some degree Abdiel's overlord and regent, one to whom the lesser angels owe a limited obedience. On the other hand, Abdiel already enjoys a higher freedom than the specious one offered by Satan. There is no hesitation in Abdiel's rejection of Satan's putative authority—putative since through rebellion Satan has severed any ties of reciprocal loyalty between himself and the upright angel serving God—or in his defiant justification of the Father. Abdiel is what Satan should have been, courageous in standing up for what he knows is right, relying on an instinctive and experiential understanding rather than on flawed, speculative reasoning. By defying Satan, Abdiel manifests the propriety, and indeed the perfection, of his choice.

The passages in which Abdiel appears are short and apparently divorced from the major movements of the epic. After Abdiel's outburst against the usurper, Satan orders him to depart, and in a flush of over-confidence and derision instructs him to relate the proceedings of the rebel Council to the Father, seemingly unaware or unwilling to believe that the Omniscient is already fully cognizant not only of the rebellion but also of the final outcome. Abdiel returns alone from the North and upon his return stands before the Father to receive His approbation.

This seeming digression, however, is actually quite essential to the progression of *Paradise Lost*. Later, Raphael's mission to Adam and Eve is to prepare them for temptations to come, and within the boundaries of that commandment to him, Raphael is free to choose the means by which to achieve his purpose. He uses Abdiel's experiences to provide Adam and Eve with a pattern by which they might recognize and repel temptation. Abdiel's situation parallels Eve's, and thus Raphael's portrait of the freely obedient angel is intended to supplement those powers already in Eve which should support her against the wiles of Satan.[90] Abdiel's experiences remind Adam and Eve that all rational beings are free to withstand the blandishments and threats of Satan and to retain that true liberty which willing obedience to the Father may alone ensure. Indeed, when the Father publicly acknowledges Abdiel's loyalty, He states:

> for this was all thy care
> To stand approv'd in sight of God, though Worlds
> Judg'd thee perverse....
>
> (*PL,* VI, 35-37)

Abdiel is Milton's most obvious model of freedom of choice among the unfallen angels, but he is not the only one. In many instances in *Paradise Lost* in which loyal angels appear individually, there is some reference to or manifestation of freedom. Raphael's mission to the prelapsarian Adam and Eve—beyond its didactic purpose of providing a pattern for righteous choice—is itself a study in initiative and alternatives. Raphael is to instruct the pair in the repercussions of past choices and adumbrate the consequences of future choices. The means by which he accomplishes this, however, are largely left up to Raphael. When Adam requests information concerning the rebellion and fall of the angels, Raphael momentarily hesitates, apparently weighing alternatives, before responding:

> Sad task and hard, for how shall I relate
> To human sense th' invisible exploits
> Of warring Spirits; how without remorse
> The ruin of so many glorious once
> And perfet while they stood; how last unfold
> The secrets of another World, *perhaps*

---

[90] Revard, "Eve and the Doctrine of Responsibility," p. 78.

> *Not lawful to reveal*? yet for thy good
> This is dispens't....
>
> (*PL*, V, 564-571; italics mine)

Raphael's hesitation, internal debate, and final decision to proceed reflect the Father's initial commandment to the angel that he should

> such discourse bring on,
> As may advise [Adam] of his happy state,
> Happiness in his power left free to will.
>
> (*PL*, V, 233-235)

Not only is Adam to be warned and strengthened in his freedom to choose, lest he willfully transgress and subsequently condemn the Father for not forewarning him, but the wording of the commandment given to Raphael is itself ambiguous and indirect, requiring the messenger to act with initiative and imagination. As with the Son's offer to serve as Mediator for man and Abdiel's courageous decision to return to the Father, Raphael's completion of his mission involves a complex balancing of freedom, responsibility, and obedience.

Gabriel's actions in guarding Eden from encroaching evil also suggest the freedom of alternative enjoyed by obedient angels. Gabriel is assigned to protect Adam and Eve until they are ready to confront directly the temptations of Satan; how he does this, however, is his choice. He positions his subordinates as need requires: Uzziel to the South, others to the North, and Ithuriel and Zephon into the Garden itself. As he sees his guards returning with Satan, he warns those about him of an impending clash with the "faded" Archangel. Again the reader views obedience confronting temptation, rage, and license. As the dialogue between Gabriel and Satan grows more and more heated, both become convinced that only warfare can settle the issue. Both are prepared for a cosmic struggle which might have rent, "disturb'd, and torn/With violence of this conflict" Paradise, the "Starry Cope of Heaven" and the elements themselves. At the last moment, however, Gabriel perceives the Scales of God weighing himself and Satan. Bowing to the will of the Father, Gabriel relinquishes any thought of battle and releases his captive. Satan is equally aware of his impotence in the face of the Father's power, and is for once unwilling to pretend otherwise; he flees, taking with him the "shades of night."

In *The Christian Doctrine*, Milton defines the angels' freedom to choose individually, as well as their collective concern that mankind also learn righteous choice:

> It seems reasonable...to suppose that the good angels stand by their own strength, no less than man did before his fall, and that they are called "elect" only in the sense that they are beloved or choice; also that they desire to contemplate the mystery of our salvation simply out of love, and not from any interest of their own, that they are not included in any question of reconciliation, and that they are reckoned as being under Christ because he is their head, not their Redeemer. (*CD*, I, ix, 345)

Through a love related to that by which Christ could offer to restore man, the angels desire to understand how man might arrive at that perfection in which the loyal angels have been confirmed.

In general, then, Milton's unfallen angels are models of true choice for man. Through apprehending the results of the angels' choices, man may learn best how to choose properly. Erasmus had suggested that the loyal angels were so strengthened in their uncorrupted will and reason "that it became henceforth impossible for them to choose evil."[91] Milton would have agreed in essence with Erasmus. For him the loyal angels are free to choose as they will; yet they will not choose other than according to the desires of the Father. Their freedom to choose is inviolable and perfect. Only through absolute obedience to absolute righteousness is such perfection possible, and the angels are indeed "absolutely obedient to the Father in all things" (*CD*, I, ix, 345).

---

[91] Winter, p. 22.

iii. Satan and the Fallen Angels

Milton was clear in his conviction that not all angels had retained their initial perfection:

> There are...both good and evil angels. Luke ix. 26 and viii. 2, for it is well known that a great many of them revolted from God of their own free will before the fall of man....
>
> Their chief is the author of all wickedness and hinders all good....
>
> As a result he has been given a number of titles, which suit his actions. He is frequently called *Satan*, that is, enemy or adversary, Job i, 6, I Chron. xxi, 1; also *the great dragon, the old serpent, the devil,* that is the calumniator.... (*CD*, I, ix, 343, 349, 350)

Just as the angels celestial define and exemplify proper choice, so the angels infernal provide an archetype of false choice. In their fall, they crystallize the contrasts between Heaven and Hell, purity and sin. Erasmus had concluded that before the revolt of Lucifer and his followers, all angels had uncorrupted wills and uncorrupted reasons. If those who remained loyal were so confirmed in their obedience that it became absolute, however, then conversely, "in those angels who fell, the will was so completely corrupted that they could not perform any meritorious acts."[92] Milton would probably have approved of Erasmus's statement, since his own devils and demons are irrevocably dedicated to evil. In *Paradise Lost*, for example, as Beelzebub reveals Satan's proposal to

> confound the race
> Of mankind in one root, and Earth with Hell
> To mingle and involve, done all to spite
> The great Creator,

---

[92] Winter, p. 22.

(*PL*, II, 382-385)

the rebellious angels heartily concur with the plan:

> The bold design
> Pleas'd highly those infernal States, and joy
> Sparkl'd in all thir eyes; with full assent
> They vote....
>
> (*PL*, II, 386-389)

As Christ and the loyal angels had defined unfallen obedience, Satan and his "Damned Crew" define the irredeemably fallen creature. As such, they reveal the extent to which fall and degradation are the consequences of improper choices; they define negatively the possibility of restoration through repentance and reconciliation with God; and finally, they provide unwitting tools by which a prescient God brings forth good from evil.

Milton constantly emphasizes both the justice of the Father and the freedom of His creatures. Satan's choice to fall is a prime example of both. Milton's contemporary, the Cambridge Platonist Benjamin Whichcote, had insisted that evil exists because God created "second causes" or "rational and voluntary beings" who are free moral agents capable of choosing evil as well as good:

> Since God is not the author of evil, the greatest evil that we encounter may be our own fault or attributed to other second causes, that is, other men or fallen angels.[93]

Whichcote assumed the freedom of Satan and the fallen angels to participate willingly in evil.

Milton's God, like Whichcote's, does not delude Satan. Instead, He allows Satan to deceive himself through false choice. Satan, persevering in those choices, destroys himself. The more he chooses counter to the desires of Heaven, the less capable he is of under-

---

[93] Roberts, p. 96.

standing God. The society which the devils establish at Pandemonium, for example, is not the same as that which Heaven had offered but is rather a parody and travesty of righteousness. The magnificence of Pandemonium suggests tyranny, idolatry, and indolent luxury, but not true civility. As an image of its creators, Pandemonium is essentially a statement of perverted freedom, a vicious metaphor for Satan's desire to imitate and subvert the will of Heaven. Its splendor is specious, its pastimes vain and empty.

In assessing Satan, it is important to remember, as Steadman has shown, that the devils fall "entirely through a 'principium internum' without the influence of any 'externo principio'...."[94] In his pride and willfulness, Satan turns from God to himself, "not wishing to be a subject, but to rejoice like a tyrant in having subjects of his own."[95] The choices Satan dares to make define process of his rebellion, fall, and final degradation.

The degradation of Satan in *Paradise Lost* becomes apparent in Book II, during the confrontation at Hell-Gate, when the reader learns that Satan had committed incest while still in Heaven. In terms of the narrative structure of the epic, the episode at Hell-Gate does provide the first overt suggestions of the evil which is in Satan and which begins to tarnish the ostensible grandeur with which he is enveloped in Pandemonium. On the other hand, the beginning diminution in magnificence which Satan experiences at Hell-Gate is equally attributable to his nearer proximity to the outer world. Although still in Hell, he is no longer speaking from the depths of darkness where he shines as the greatest of the rebels. He is approaching nearer to the Father's goodness—after all, Sin and Death have been appointed guardians of the Gate by God—and consequently, the reader begins to see in Satan the devil he has become. The revelation of Satan's incest emphasizes the alterations in his character which accompany his descent from Archangel to devil.

The confrontation clarifies Satan's role in Milton's universe. Self-directed, introverted, and anxious to protect his own esteem,

---

[94] John M. Steadman, "The Causal Structure of the Fall," *JHI*, 21 (1960), p. 185.

[95] Lewis, p. 66.

glory, and pride, Satan provides a paradigm of the traditional martial hero, a model which *Paradise Lost* and *Paradise Regained* both invalidate. His relationship to Sin and Death amplifies his perversion of heroism; Satan, setting out to destroy, not preserve, life, confronts his own creations, Sin and Death. Sin clearly states her progeniture: as Satan had presided at the Assembly of the rebels,

> All on a sudden miserable pain
> Surpris'd thee, dim thine eyes, and dizzy swum
> In darkness, while thy head flames thick and fast
> Threw forth, till on the left side op'ning wide,
> Likest to thee in shape and count'nance bright,
> Then shining heav'nly fair, a Goddess arm'd
> Out of thy head I sprung....
>
> (*PL*, II, 752-758)

Key words in the passage are "miserable pain" (presumably the first felt in Heaven, and thus the first external manifestation of imperfection), "dim thine eyes," "Darkness," and "flames," all presaging Satan's future experiences in Hell. The bringing forth of Sin, parodying as it does the birth of the Goddess of Wisdom from the brow of Jupiter, suggests the most important meanings of the episode. Satan produces Sin from within himself, during the Assembly in which he initiates the rebellion. Sin is thus the first result of Satan's choice to rebel. She is the logical consequence of his free actions. She emerges from within him rather than imposing herself upon him externally. And, as with all false choices, she imprisons him (later—and literally—in Hell) and limits the possibility of alternative choice, until the will of Heaven permits him to leave.

Similarly, Death is a result of Satan's freedom of choice. Having conceived of Sin while still in Heaven (although rebellious and soon to fall), Satan even further defies moral law. According to Sin,

> familiar grown,
> I pleas'd, and with attractive graces won
> The most averse, thee chiefly, who full oft
> Thyself in me thy perfect image viewing

> Becam'st enamor'd, and such joy thou took'st
> With me in secret, that my womb conceiv'd
> A growing burden.
>
> <div align="right">(<i>PL</i>, II, 761-767)</div>

This passage suggests a perversion of the Father's creative love for the Son, His image. The creativity that characterizes the Father is here turned to narcissistic self-love and destructive incest. Satan proposes to destroy "upstart" man by releasing Sin and Death upon the earth, yet paradoxically, through the mediation of the Son, the proper image of God's love, Death shall finally bind and limit Satan irrevocably. Satan's own illicit progeny shall be his ultimate undoing.

Thus from the beginning moments of his rebellion, Satan's choices have set him on a path leading to confinement, limitation, and spiritual death. Satan's choice to rebel while still in Heaven results in his disfigurement and fall; his further decision to persevere in that rebellion necessitates for him his final state—abandonment to Sin and Death, concretizations of his own perverted reason and lust. Satan has no one else to blame for his fallen state. As the Hell-Gate episode clearly shows, Satan alone sired Sin and Death; he alone is responsible for their entering the universe.

The rebellion and fall of Satan and the disloyal angels depends upon free choices by those involved. The initial act of rebellion is accomplished in Satan's turning from God to self. Joined in his error by those whom he persuades to follow him in willfully denying their better knowledge (and Abdiel's defense indicates that the facts of creation were known to all of the angels), Satan defies God.

During the War in Heaven, the hand-to-hand combats, flyting, and heroic taunts partially convince the reader that Satan's braggadocio may have some foundation in truth. The principal combatants, Satan and Michael, seem equal and in fact represent equivalent orders of creation. Against the other, neither can make much headway, even when Satan resorts to such dishonorable extremes as inventing gunpowder. Only with the arrival of the Son does it become clear that Satan and his hosts are vulnerable. They still retain powers God originally bestowed upon them, for without those powers the principle of free choice would cease to exist.

By the time the rebels are forced from Heaven, however—not by a classical clash of arms but purely by the inherently invincible power of the Son—they have refused at least three times to alter their decisions: once when invited to withdraw with Satan to the North; again when Satan openly proclaimed rebellion from the heights of his imitative throne; and finally when actual warfare began. As Abdiel's case illustrates, the rebels could have returned to obedience and rejected Satan's pride-inspired perversions, yet only one of the angels caught up in Satan's host chose to do so. The others persisted in their choices and perforce suffered the consequences of obduracy. Satan and his host subsequently cease to be angels; their names are "heard no more in Heav'n." Through their choices now and in Hell, they imbrute themselves farther and farther from God, until finally, in Book X, they are no longer Angels of Light, but hissing serpents.

Having fallen, Satan and the devils construct Pandemonium, an external, concrete manifestation of Satan's urge to destruction and sterility. A Grand Council convenes, ostensibly for the purpose of acting against the Deity. Yet there is no true, unhampered choice possible for the Infernal Council. Having decided to abet Satan in rebellion, the devils have voluntarily relinquished their right and ability to choose. The façade of choice which Satan allows the Council dissolves into politic trickery and theatrical manipulation on the parts of Satan and Beelzebub.

According to Satan, his leadership is based on traditional sanctions: reason, the law of God, free elections, and pre-eminence among warriors (*PL,* II, 18-24). The fallen angels, however, are incapable of perceiving the truth behind Satan's arrogations. They have given up their freedom, having chosen disobedience to the perfect righteousness of Heaven, and no longer understand that Satan's claims to authority are specious. The "fixt laws of Heav'n" establish the Father and His Son as the leaders of all created beings. Free choice does not exist in Hell, since Satan knows in advance what he proposes to do and how to do it. Yet not even he realizes that he is acting purely through the permissive will of the Father. Nor does

Satan, as angel though fallen, have the ability to perform more meritorious actions than others of his sort—indeed, Abdiel (whose name in fact means 'servant of God') has achieved much more "In Council or in Fight...of merit" than has Satan and the devils. The rebels are blind to all of these truths. Since no true alternative can exist in Hell, the farthest extreme from the freedom of Heaven, their only recourse is to follow Satan blindly in what their new tyrant "chooses" to do.

Politic though he may be, Satan is basically unaware of the ironies inherent in his own pretensions. He goes through the motions of heroic activity, not realizing that he, like Achilles, Turnus, and other archetypal heroes of traditional martial epics, has revealed his selfishness and desire for personal reputation and glory. He willingly accepts the forced accolade of the hosts before him (*PL*, II, 473-482), but in reality he is venturing nothing since there is nothing left for him to lose, having rejected obedience to the Father in favor of self-gratification. And after Satan departs, the fallen angels are left completely leaderless, idly passing their time in useless activity, in "wand'ring mazes lost."

Through their decisions and actions during the rebellion, the fallen angels give their freedoms over to Satan's control and cease to be heroic in any sense of the term. Ironically, Satan is exalted to eminence because his proposal is ostensibly superior to the others presented; yet Satan himself does not realize that his plan is the only one by which the inhabitants of Hell might in fact fall even lower than their present state. Only when Satan voluntarily degrades himself by entering the form of the Serpent does the Father decree serpentine forms as just punishment for all inhabitants of Hell.

In addition, Satan's proposal incorporates unwittingly critical points suggested by other devils. Moloch had spoken out for open warfare; ultimately Satan's plan will result in a face-to-face confrontation between Satan and Christ, detailed in *Paradise Regained*. Belial had urged conscious subservience to the superior power of Heaven; Satan and his crew become the unconscious tools of the Father, subservient to His will. Mammon had drawn attention to the "hidden lustre, Gems and Gold" (II, 271) which the devils might use to counterfeit Heaven; and as Satan confronts the Son in *Paradise*

Regained, one of his first ploys is to tempt Christ with a counterfeit kingdom founded on gold (*PR,* II, 426-429). Finally, Beelzebub's plan (and Satan's) had plotted the destruction of another of God's creatures; in attempting to accomplish that, however, Satan brings about the degradation and further enslavement of himself and of the infernal angels who follow him. The entire Council scene thus accentuates the increasing limitation and final destruction of the freedom once enjoyed in Heaven by the rebels. Each action they take, each decision they reach further condemns them to a deeper Hell of their own creation.

One of the perennial complaints about Milton's treatment of Satan in *Paradise Lost* and *Paradise Regained* is that the poet, apparently discovering the majesty with which he had invested his villain, arbitrarily degrades him through the course of Books III-XII. In order to account for Milton's portrayal of Satan as the source of all lies and deceit, and his emphasis on Satan's dedication to absolute evil, some critics have re-interpreted *Paradise Lost* and have suggested that Satan is the true hero, seduced by the Father into rebellion.

In a romanticization of Satan, E. E. Stoll faults Milton for failing to prove Satan's evil and attempts to justify Satan's actions. According to Stoll, Satan's boasts of having confounded Heaven and shaken the Throne of God must be either self-deception or lying; and Stoll prefers to believe that Satan is thoroughly deceived by God and thus believes in the lie of his own power and near-omnipotence, is justified in his rebellion, and ultimately triumphs over defeat.[96]

William Empson similarly asserts that Satan was ignorant of the basic truth that he was rebelling against omnipotence: "...Satan did not believe he was attacking omnipotence; and the other angels would not have followed him if he had done." Satan is deluded by God into false choices and illusory alternatives. Empson justifies Satan's rebellion by concluding that God, in deluding Satan, has convinced the fallen Archangel that Hell is the honest side of the argument and that Satan's choice to rebel is necessary in order to uphold the hierarchy of the universe.[97]

---

[96] E. E. Stoll, "Give the Devil His Due," *RES*, o.s. XX (1944), 108-124.

[97] William Empson, "Milton's God," *Listener*, 64 (1960), pp. 11-12.

Taking Empson's justification of Satan one step further, Richmond claims that Milton used Satan to express his own disappointment at political failure. After comparing Moloch with the final stage of the Third Reich, at least in terms of psychological defeat, Richmond claims that

> Like Satan, Milton had expected to enforce the superiority of his own political vision upon the whole English nation, but also like Satan had found himself cast down into hellish darkness, in despair of all future success. His refuge similarly lies in finding a way to preserve his fading and subjective vision.... To claim solipsistically that one speaks with authority for God is natural and ominous compensation for a failing politician.[98]

Satan thus primarily becomes an image of the poet, an image retreating into self-aggrandizement as compensation for unjust defeat.

Unfortunately, a single underlying fallacy mars each of these several approaches. In addition to C. S. Lewis's remark that much of the modern controversy over Satan results from the fact that Milton

> did not foresee that his work would one day meet the disarming simplicity of critics who take for gospel things said by the father of falsehood in public speeches to his troops,[99]

a more serious charge against such views as those of Stoll, Empson, and Richmond is that they negate Milton's emphasis on Satan's free choice of rebellion over obedience. Milton quite carefully shows that Satan's fall, degradation, and final punishments are the results of choices and decisions freely entered into by the Father of Lies. Satan decrees in large measure his own doom. He chooses to invest his

---

[98] Richmond, p. 136.
[99] Lewis, p. 100.

angelic matter with the forms of earthly creatures, apparently thereby coarsening and lessening his original nature.

After the Father and the Son conclude the Divine Council of Book III, Milton moves with the reader to the arrival of Satan at the Paradise of Fools and introduces Satan with an epic simile describing him as a "Vultur on *Imaus* bred" a highly appropriate image for one whose progeny is Death and whose purpose is to gorge and glut himself on the souls of men. Then, later, as Satan approaches Eden, he is describes as a "prowling Wolf," and "this first grand Thief" climbing into "God's Fold." His first act within the Garden is to fly to the highest tree of the Garden, the Tree of Life, and sit "like a Cormorant" devising death. From this height, itself an image of his earlier arrogation of unmerited height and dignity in Books I and II, Satan descends voluntarily to assume a variety of forms, the more easily to insinuate himself closer to Eve. He becomes a Lion, then a Tiger crouching near Adam and Eve. Finally, as Ithuriel and Zephon discover him, he is "Squat like a Toad" next to Eve's ear.

In each instance, Satan's ignoble disguise is a perversion of the conventional epic noble disguise, a diminishing of his claims to heroism, and a demeaning of his angelic essence as it assumes increasingly brutish—and quite literally 'lower'—forms. The various animals each suggest elements of Satan's personality: greed, lust, and violence, culminating in the batrachian image of "like a Toad." This diminishing of the heroic is carried out further in Book IX, in which Satan again attempts to enter Eden, this time as a "rising Mist." In Eden, he selects the beast which "Most opportune might serve his Wiles," the "fittest Imp of fraud": the Serpent (*PL*, IX, 85, 90), the lowest of the beasts of the field.

Satan does not relinquish entirely the angelic prowess that had once been his. In Book IV, for example, Milton reminds the reader that the fallen Archangel is still possibly capable of bringing not only Paradise, but also "the starry cope/Of Heav'n perhaps, or all the elements" to ruin through the threatened violence of his encounter with Gabriel (992-993). In general, however, Lewis is correct when he notes that Satan gradually regresses from "hero to general, from general to politician, from politician to secret agent, and thence to a thing that peers in at bedroom or bathroom windows, and thence to a toad, and finally to a snake,"[100] each stage being the irrevocable result of a choice freely made. Satan intends to further the destruction of man, but instead unknowingly determines his own fate.

When Satan returns to Hell in Book X, he seems again to radiate grandeur and greatness, but only because he is once more on his home soil. The creature who has been successively bird of prey, carnivore, amphibian, and serpentine tempter is no longer capable of the illusion of brightness anywhere except against the backdrop of the absolute darkness of Hell. Then, even as he is speaking, this illusion of glory also shatters as the Father's judgments decree for Satan and his Crew the form that his choices make just. Prior to their transformation, the devils assemble as if they were not changed, as if they were still angels and archangels conversant with the intimate joys of Heaven. Yet an essential alteration has taken place. Even as Satan concludes the report of his success, the consequences of unbridled freedom of choice descend upon the assembled demons:

> So having said, a while he stood, expecting
> This universal shout and high applause
> To fill his ear, when contrary he hears
> On all sides, from innumerable tongues
> A dismal universal hiss, the sound
> Of public scorn....
>   ...down he fell
> A monstrous Serpent on his Belly prone,
> Reluctant, but in vain: a greater power
> Now rul'd him, punisht in the shape he sinn'd,
> According to his doom....
>   (*PL*, X, 504-509, 513-517)

The devils, who had earlier applauded Satan's proposal to gain mankind for Hell, now share with their leader his just punishment. Their final condemnation is irrevocable and consistent with the Father's concern for freedom of choice. The fallen angels had made

---

[100] Lewis., p. 98.

their decisions to follow Satan; they must now accept the responsibility and punishment which accompany false choice.

The fall of Satan and the inhabitants of Hell was self-determined and largely self-imposed. For that reason Milton explicitly denies the possibility of their regeneration. As early as the writings of Clement of Alexandria and of Origen, theologians had speculated on the applicability to Satan of the principle of *Apocatastasis*, the restoration of all things as spoken of in the New Testament.[101] In his speech on Mount Niphates, Satan himself confronts this question:

> Which way I fly is Hell; myself am Hell;
> And in the lowest deep a lower deep
> Still threat'ning to devour me opens wide,
> To which the Hell I suffer seems a Heav'n.
> O then at last relent; is there no place
> Left for Repentance, none for Pardon left?
> (*PL*, IV, 75-80)

Satan's answer is negative on two counts. First, the nature of Satan's crime is such as to preclude the possibility of re-admission into Heaven. In *Paradise Lost*, Book V, after proclaiming the begetting of the Son and commanding absolute obedience to him, the Father had declared that

> him who disobeys
> Mee disobeys, breaks union, and that day
> Cast out from God and blessed vision, falls
> Into utter darkness, deep ingulft, his place
> Ordain'd without redemption, without end.
> (*PL*, V, 611-615)

The Father had further decreed the rebel angels' unmitigated punishment a second time when, in describing the context and results of the fall of Adam and Eve, He states:

---

[101] Patrides, "The Salvation of Satan," *JHI*, XXVIII (1967), p. 467; see also Evans, p. 179.

> they themselves ordain'd thir fall.
> The first sort by thir own suggestion fell,
> Self-tempted, self-depriv'd: Man falls deceiv'd
> By th' other first: Man therefore shall find grace,
> The other none....
>
> *(PL,* III, 128-131)

Without grace, coupled with correct choice and concomitant works, there can be no restoration. Satan and his angels are expelled for the crime of conscious rebellion against the vice-gerent of Heaven. As spiritual beings who had denied their intuitive and experiential knowledge, they are condemned for their false choice, regardless of their rationalization of it.

The second and most telling argument (particularly in view of Milton's emphasis on moral choice) is simply that Satan would *choose* not to repent, even if the opportunity for repentance were given him. His attitude toward God allows only for further degradation. Their demonic inversion of foreknowledge plays the same role in Hell as divine foreknowledge does on earth; it does not necessitate, but it does foresee. Satan's boast,

> Here we may reign secure, and in my choice
> To reign is worth ambition though in Hell:
> Better to reign in Hell, than serve in Heav'n,
>
> *(PL,* I, 261-263)

explicitly states that he *wants* to continue in his rebellion.

On Mount Niphates, Satan must determine the possibility of repentance and restoration. He knows intellectually and experientially that the angels were created with freedom of choice and that obedience forced is not true obedience. Satan knows that his misery is self-inflicted and accepts the responsibility for it. His attitude toward repentance can lead only to his own further enslavement. As a fallen being, in spiritual bondage, with his understanding darkened by obduracy in conscious sin, Satan repeatedly denies the goodness of

God and chooses instead a selfish, peevishly perverted path. As a consequence, he and those with him are irrevocably condemned.

In spite of his spiritual bondage, however, Satan is allowed great freedom of mobility physically in both *Paradise Lost* and *Paradise Regained*. If, as has been indicated, Satan is wholly evil and reprobate of his own volition, what justification can there be for God allowing him to extend his corruption throughout other levels of creation? Milton's answer is that Satan, having defied what he believed to be the limiting strictures of God's laws, has surrendered his freedom and become the unconscious tool of the Father.

Many readers have noted that God's attitude toward Satan is basically ironic; as Satan becomes the personification of evil, God uses him as a tool for the creation of greater good than Satan is able to pervert. Such a view was a commonplace in the seventeenth century, as a passage from Christopher Lever's *The Holy Pilgrim* (1618) indicates:

> The divels have neither liberty nor pleasure, but being fettered with limitations, cannot doe what they would, but what they are only licenced. The angels are God's servants, but the divels are his slaves; both labour in his works, but with great inequalitie.[102]

Milton parallels this interpretation of the function of Satan and the demons. In *Paradise Lost*, whatever Satan does is through the permissive will of Heaven. His rising from the flames in Hell is the result solely of divine permission (I, 209-213); his role in the War in Heaven is foreseen (VI, 674-675); he is allowed to enter Paradise (III, 523-535); and even his progeny Sin and Death cross the abyss only with Heaven's permission (II, 1025; X, 622-624).

Satan's dependence upon divine permission is even more explicit in *Paradise Regained*. His long speech to the concourse of devils in Book I is ostensibly a paean to the powers and authority of Satan on earth; in actuality, however, it is a devastatingly ironic pre-

---

[102] Cited in Patrides, "Milton and His Contemporaries on the Chains of Satan," *MLN*, 73 (1968), pp. 258-259.

sumption of limited abilities which have been granted by God. The powers of which he boasts have been lent for the express purpose of furthering the damnation of Satan and his angels and making possible the redemption of man. When Satan boasts of leaving his "dolorous Prison" to move freely throughout the Earth and, indeed, to enter Heaven itself (I, 363-367), Christ responds with the following indictment:

> thou com'st indeed,
> As a poor miserable captive thrall
> Comes to the place where he before had sat
> Among the Prime in Splendor, now depos'd,
> Ejected, emptied, gaz'd, unpitied, shunn'd,
> A spectacle of ruin or of scorn
> To all the Hosts of Heaven; the happy place
> Imparts to thee no happiness, no joy,
> Rather inflames thy torment, representing
> Lost bliss, to thee no more communicable,
> So never more in Hell than when in Heaven.
> (*P.R.*, I, 410-420)

Satan's much-vaunted freedom of movement, like his apparent freedom of choice, is illusory. By choosing rebellion over obedience, he has subjected himself to the laws of God and rejected the freedom inherent in God's mercy and grace. His express goal of perverting all good to evil is reversed to the unknowing creation of good out of apparent evil. Satan is intellectually aware of the powers of God, but chooses not to accept that knowledge, striving instead against true reason. God allows him to do this in order to fulfill two objectives. The first, and least important, is the willful degradation of Satan and his followers (*PL*, I, 211-216). Through their efforts at spreading the contagion of disobedience, Satan and his "Damned Crew" become the instruments of their own damnation. The second objective is to implement the redemption of man through the Son: Satan,

> enrag'd might see

> How all his malice serv'd but to bring forth
> Infinite goodness, grace and mercy shown
> On Man by him seduc't, but on himself
> Treble confusion, wrath and vengeance pour'd.
>
> (*PL*, I, 216-220)

Through the loyal angels' choices to remain obedient to God, man may learn faithfulness. Through the rebels' choices to turn from God, man may understand unfaithfulness. But more than that, through the rebellion of Satan and his followers, the machinery for man's ultimate restoration with God is put into motion.

For Milton and for his Adam, and for all humanity to follow, there is only one true pattern of obedience and freedom—the absolute adherence to righteous choice exemplified by Christ, Abdiel, and the loyal angels. On the other hand, there are many patterns of false choice, many paths which lead to disobedience and away from God. Throughout his poetry, Milton defines those multiform paths and tries to dissuade man from attempting them. The single path to obedience leads to fullest life and freedom; the many paths of disobedience lead—as Satan and his Crew illustrate—only to limitation and death.

CHAPTER SIX

Man in Eden—
Choice and Consequence

> It was necessary that one thing at least should be either forbidden or commanded, and above all something which was in itself neither good nor evil, so that man's obedience might this way be made evident. For man was by nature good and holy, and was naturally disposed to do right, so it was certainly not necessary to bind him by the requirements of any covenant to do something which he would do of his own accord.
>
> —*The Christian Doctrine*, I, x

i. Man's Responsibility for Sin

Milton's strong sense of vocation apparently impelled not only his need to understand God and the Heavenly Spheres (as far as was humanly possible), but also and more importantly the need to define the relationships between those celestial levels and this earth. For Milton, humanity was a creation of the Father, and thus, like the Son and the angels, participated in the flow of freedom and choice which reached outward from the Father. Milton's concern for correctly assessing the role of man in the universe was so strong that at least one critic, John C. Ulreich, has argued that any coherence in *Paradise Lost* ultimately depends upon Milton's examination of the Fall of

Man, not upon his representation of the mock-rebellion or of the truly heroic offer of the Son. The allusion to "Man's First Disobedience" in the first line is an essential key to understanding the epic.[103] Christ may be the only character who is by strict definition heroic; Satan may be the archetype of villainy and (as often appears) the most vital and energetic character—but the circumstances surrounding the Fall of Man provide the structure and organization of Milton's thinking. As "parent and head of all men," Adam

> either stood or fell as a representative of the whole human race; this was true both when the covenant was made, that is, when he received God's command, and also when he sinned. (*CD*, I, ix, 384-385)

Consequently, Milton felt it necessary to establish clearly man's responsibility for that sin.

In emphasizing Adam's freedom of choice, Milton drew from a long tradition. Irenaeus stated that "God has always preserved freedom and the power of self-government in man." Origen saw evil as introduced into the world as a consequence of the sins decided upon and committed by man. Lactantius taught that man's freedom was in part confirmed by the temptation itself and "that God did not consign Satan to immediate punishment at the time of the primal transgression because, without Satan's temptation, man would lack the means of strengthening and perfecting his virtue."[104] For Lactantius, as later for Milton, man was a creature capable of intelligent, rational, and moral strengthening through unimpeded choice.

Milton also shared beliefs with writers closer to his own time. Erasmus had argued that both Adam and Eve were created with a will so good that they could have remained in a state of innocence without additional grace, although only through Christ could they have attained eternal life.[105] Their choice to fall was consequently a

---

[103] John C. Ulreich, "'Sufficient to Have Stood': Adam's Responsibility in Book IX," *MQ*, V, 2 (May 1971), p. 38.

[104] James Barker, pp. 46, 201.

[105] Winter, p. 22.

perversion of their free and almost perfect will. In addition, as Steadman notes, in removing the onus of initiating human sin and placing it upon man, Milton is in harmony with Melanchthon, Ames, and Wolleb.[106] Among Milton's contemporaries, the Cambridge Platonists were particularly emphatic in their estimate of man's freedom. More's *Conjectura Cabbalistica* describes the soul of man as "so free, so rational, and so intellectual."[107] Whichcote argued that "man is in a probation state and is necessarily free and for this reason evil is unavoidable…. Evil results from man's choices."[108] Merit or demerit can result only from the unrestrained exercise of man's will toward good or evil.

Milton thus fits into a strong tradition when he endows his newly created man and woman with a freedom of choice capable of withstanding temptations. Man's freedom is an essential part of his spiritual and physical make-up, a quality which enables man ultimately to fulfill the potentialities inherent in him from his creation. The fall is thus a violation and perversion of man's true nature—of that end for which man was created. Man is created "sufficient to have stood, though free to fall" (*PL*, III, 99).

The Father foreknew the fall of man, of course, as Milton clearly indicates in *The Christian Doctrine*:

> The principal SPECIAL DECREE of God which concerns men is called PREDESTINATION: by which GOD, BEFORE THE FOUNDATIONS OF THE WORLD WERE LAID, HAD MERCY ON THE HUMAN RACE, ALTHOUGH IT WAS GOING TO FALL OF ITS OWN ACCORD, AND, TO SHOW THE GLORY OF HIS MERCY, GRACE AND WISDOM, PREDESTINED TO ETERNAL SALVATION, ACCORDING TO HIS PURPOSE or plan IN CHRIST, THOSE WHO WOULD IN THE

---

[106] Steadman, "The Causal Structure of the Fall," p. 193.
[107] Nicolson, "Milton and the *Conjectura Cabbalistica*," p. 8.
[108] Roberts, p. 96-97.

FUTURE BELIEVE AND CONTINUE IN THE FAITH. (*CD*, I, iv, p. 168)

> The matter or object of predestination was not simply man who was to be created, but man who was going to fall of his own free will.
> (*CD*, I, iv, p. 173)

In order for Milton to succeed in his theodicy, he had to absolve God of guilt in "Man's First Disobedience." Adam must be primarily responsible, and the punishment for the sin must be correct. In *Paradise Lost*, the Father defines man as a free agent, capable of unnecessitated choice. Through Satan's deceit, man will be seduced

> And flatter'd out of all, believing lies
> Against his Maker; no Decree of mine
> Concurring to necessitate his Fall,
> Or touch with lightest moment of impulse
> His free Will, to her own inclining left
> In even scale.
> (*PL*, X, 42-47)

After admitting the complicity of Satan in seducing man, Milton places the primary burden of guilt on man. There is no hint Adam was not absolutely free to choose other than he ultimately did.

If one divides attention for a moment and considers Adam and Eve separately, Milton's treatment of the human pair becomes clear. Although created to be a unit, and joined in marriage (*PL*, VIII, 484-489), they each function, as all beings do, as individuals. Each is endowed with a birthright of choice; each must make decisions and be responsible for the consequences.

In the *Areopagitica*, Milton refutes those who would deny Adam freedom of action and choice and would make of Adam a puppet-man completely controlled by God. Milton argues that by denying man's freedom to choose, one must consequently impute evil to God. Yet if Adam were created perfect—and otherwise God would be responsible for creating imperfection—how could he have fallen?

Evans argues that the defection of either an innocent, child-like creature, or of a demi-god presents great difficulty, and that the introduction of free will into the problem does not help very much, since one would expect a perfect being to choose the good.[109] Milton, however, sees that freedom of the will is the *only* possible answer. Adam is not a statically, immutably perfect individual, nor is he an unlearned innocent adrift in the world. He is a dynamic individual, constantly changing through the decisions he makes. Adam is expected to make correct choices and to remain faithful to the will of the Father and to the potential for righteous choice inherent in human nature. If anything diverts him from following these two prime objectives, man will fail to achieve his full stature. At a critical point, Adam allows inferior motives to hamper his awareness of the good—and he falls.

If Adam's fall results from making false choices counter to his better knowledge, so does Eve's. Eve is as free an agent as Adam. Adam is subject to the Father, and Eve is subject to him; yet just as Adam is granted freedom to choose and act by his superior, so he releases Eve from his total control. Eve is free to act according to her own knowledge. Unable to participate directly in Adam's panoramic visions of future generations, she receives comforting enlightenment in a mode no longer open fully to Adam. As Michael instructs Adam, the angel indicates the difference between man's mode of knowing the divine plan and woman's:

> Her also I with gentle Dreams have calm'd
> Portending good, and all her spirits compos'd
> To meek submission: thou at season fit
> Let her with thee partake what thou hast heard,
> Chiefly what may concern her Faith to know....
> (*PL*, XII, 595-599)

Adam learns of mankind's future directly through vision and revelation. As Eve's head, however, he is responsible for imparting to her such knowledge as she requires. Eve perceives through dreams,

---

[109] Evans, p. 23

emotion, and intuition, while Adam acts through reason. In the separation scene, for example, Adam is led by choice, while Eve will find what awaits her among the roses (*PL*, IX 214-219).

Adam and Eve differ in their modes of perception, in their justification and motivations, and in their degrees of disobedience. However, as different as the two might be, Milton nonetheless shows that they are perfectly free to act according to whatever knowledge, awareness, and desires they have. If Adam is wrong for allowing Eve her liberty of choice, then God is likewise wrong for allowing Satan to tempt Adam. Adam and Eve may unhappily fail the great test (a test different for yet appropriate to each), but they do so through the exercise of divinely sanctioned freedom.

ii. Adam and Eve in the Garden

Milton's Adam and Eve are, from the first moments of their creation, endowed with knowledge, intellect, reason, and the capacity to learn, choose, and act. Individually, and as a unit, they define Milton's concern with humankind's moral liberty, particularly as Adam and Eve make those choices which ultimately lead to disobedience and fall.

The reader's first impressions of the "Offspring of Heav'n and Earth, and all Earth's Lord" stem largely from Adam's actions and dialogues, either with Eve or with angelic messengers. Adam's own history remains obscure until his conversation with Raphael. When Raphael advises Adam to be "lowly wise:/Think only what concerns thee and thy being" (*PL*, VIII, 173-174), Adam ceases inquiring after the mysteries of Heaven and instead relates to the angel his own earliest memories.

Having just heard from Raphael the causes and results of Satan's rebellion and fall, Adam scrupulously avoids duplicating Satan's errors and denies any experiential knowledge of the creation of man (*PL*, VIII, 250-251). As a newly formed, newly conscious creation, Adam's first reacts almost purely instinctively; he rises and stands upright, taking the form intended for him by his Creator, a form physically and spiritually symbolic of his reason, intellect, and superiority to the lesser beasts (*PL*, VII, 505-516). Upon gaining a consciousness of himself and of his surroundings, Adam officially asserts the authority conferred by the Creator upon him and assigns names to objects in his world—the sun, the earth, the hills, dales, rivers, woods, and plains—drawing upon an instinctive knowledge of God (*PL*, VIII, 352-354).

Adam then sleeps and dreams that the earth becomes a Paradise Waking, he finds that this dream had presaged truth. Given dominion over the new Paradise, along with a Law forbidding tasting of the Tree of Knowledge, Adam is instructed to care for the new earth, to act as his incentive directs as Lord of the Earth and Namer of all things, and in return receives from them "fealty/With low subjection" (*PL*, VIII, 338-345). By naming the creatures, Adam establishes his superiority and sovereignty over them; yet he also acknowledges his own dependence upon God, since

> I nam'd them, as they pass'd, and understood
> Thir Nature, with such knowledge God endu'd
> My sudden apprehension....
> (*PL*, VIII, 352-354)

Through the aid of God, Adam thus fulfills the first level of his creation.

Even as he names the beasts, Adam experiences a strong feeling of isolation. Throughout his dialogue with the Creator, Adam expresses his desire for a creature nearer himself than the beasts, even though the "vision bright" suggests that Adam should be content to "Find pastime, and bear rule" among the various creatures of the earth. Adam perseveres in his request, however, and, as he explains to Raphael:

> Thus I embold'n'd spake, and *freedom us'd*
> *Permissive*, and acceptance found, which gain'd
> This answer from the gracious voice Divine.
> (*PL*, VIII, 434-436; italics mine)

Adam knows the importance of freedom of choice (in this case, represented by his decision to petition the Creator for additional bounty), and his exercise of that freedom is promptly rewarded. He is told that his desire is just, that the earlier dialogue had been a test to which Adam had correctly responded (*PL*, VIII, 444-448). Adam has successfully met his second challenge as a rational creation; he has judged correctly, thus providing himself with a pattern of choice and action upon which subsequent choices should be modeled.

In a second dream, Adam vicariously observes the creation of Eve, described in terms reminiscent of those he had used in discussing his vision of Paradise during the earlier dream (*PL*, VIII, 495-499). He names her and, significantly, recognizes that he and she form a unity. Before Eve's creation, Adam learns both directly, through vision and revelation, and indirectly, through dreams. After Eve's creation, he largely ceases to dream, depending instead on more direct, more rational ways of knowing. Eve, on the other hand, learns through dreams. Milton seems to be suggesting that before his union with Eve, Adam contained within himself the capacity to learn through a variety of means. After Eve's creation, the couple, as a unity, share access to both modes of knowing.

When Adam awakens from his second dream, he searches for the woman. Brisman points out that when Adam wakes "to find her, or forever to deplore/Her loss, and other pleasures all abjure" (VIII, 479-480), the reader is to hear in the *or* intimations of choices yet to come between loss of Eve and loss of Eden itself."[110] That is still in the future, however, and as Adam concludes his narration, he allows his passions to overpower his reason. He swells eloquent over the glories and beauties of Eve, until Raphael, with "contracted brow," warns Adam of the folly of

> ...attributing overmuch to things
> Less excellent, as thou thyself perceiv'st.
> What higher in her society thou find'st
> Attractive, human, rational, love still;
> In loving thou dost well, in passion not,
> Wherein true Love consists not....
> (*PL*, VIII, 565-566, 586-589)

---

[110] Brisman, pp. 22-23.

Briefly, then, Adam is aware of himself as a creation. He never arrogates to himself the prerogatives of a Creator, giving names, for example, only as he is inspired to do so. He faces situations in which choices are necessary, and in each case his decisions meet with God's approval. Decision and choice are not evil; improper choice alone leads to punishment. Adam is faulted only once, toward the end of his narration, when he begins to over-react to remembrance of Eve's charms; and Raphael's warnings themselves presuppose Adam's ability to reverse himself and make proper choices:

>   take heed lest Passion sway
> Thy Judgment to do aught, which else free Will
> Would not admit; thine and of all thy Sons
> The weal or woe in thee is plac't; beware.
> I in thy persevering shall rejoice,
> And all the Blest: stand fast; to stand or fall
> Free in thine own Arbitrement it lies.
> Perfet within, no outward aid require;
> And all temptation to transgress repel.
>   (*P.L.*, VIII, 635-643)

The repeated *or* clearly establishes Adam's responsibility toward himself and his yet unborn posterity: "weal or woe," "stand or fall." The choice is freely Adam's.

Eve's creation is less fully narrated than was Adam's. She speaks to Adam only of her first moments, of her reflection in the water, and of the voice which leads her to Adam. Yet even her brief outline confirms Eve's ability to choose wisely. Her initial enchantment with her own reflection implies a possible vanity, but one which—in prelapsarian Eden—is not inherently evil. When the commanding voice speaks to her, she responds immediately and correctly, however, stating "what could I do/But follow straight, invisibly led?" (*PL*, IV, 475-476). In a similar situation, Satan had failed to remove himself from self-idolatry. In Book II (761-767), Sin related Satan's incestuous passion, emphasizing her likeness to her father. Entrapped by his self-image, Satan chose to indulge in self-love, thus engendering Death. Eve easily breaks away from her reflection, on the other hand, and is led willingly to Adam, the perfect image of her Creator. Upon seeing Adam for the first time, Eve falters briefly, then approaches him in obedience to the voice. From her own beginning, Eve is demonstrably capable of free choice, each decision furthering her progress and development. Both Adam and Eve are free agents, both possessing the potential for perfect choice.

A number of readers have concluded that sin, in one form or another, seems inevitable, if not actual, in Eden, long before any definite, overt act of disobedience occurs. Any interpretation which diminishes Adam and Eve as free agents, however, contradicts Milton's view of humankind. The first parents must be free to choose and act while in Eden, since their experiences in Paradise will provide a pattern for proper and improper choices for their progeny. Adam and Eve develop through accepting the responsibility for their choices and making decisions essential to their progress. They are in a constant flux between "either" and "or," and the repercussions of each decision become increasingly severe as time passes.

Milton stresses the potential in Adam and Eve for choice and, through that choice, for change. In Book IV, for example, as Milton introduces Adam and Eve, he describes Eve:

> Shee as a veil down to the slender waist
> Her unadorned golden tresses wore
> Dishevell'd, but in wanton ringlets wav'd
> As the Vine curls her tendrils, which impli'd
> Subjection, but requir'd with gentle sway....
> <div align="right">(<i>PL</i>, IV, 304-308)</div>

In the context of Book IV, the "wanton ringlets" suggest profuseness and luxuriance, paralleling Milton's earlier description of the Garden in which Nature had "Pour'd forth profuse on Hill and Dale and Plain" flowers "worthy of Paradise" (IV, 243, 240). The alternative, pejorative meanings of *wanton* are, for the moment, overshadowed by the innocence of Eve. Later, in Book IX, Milton similarly uses *wanton* merely to suggest luxuriant growth; Eve speaks to Adam and reminds him that

> what we by day
> Lop overgrown, or prune, or prop, or bind,
> One night or two with wanton growth derides
> Tending to wild.
>
> (209-212)

Still later, however, as Eve watches the Serpent curling "many a wanton wreath" before her (IX, 517), Milton shows that there are other, more dangerous, meanings to the word and that Eve is now being introduced to them. Finally, as Eve "wantonly" repays the fallen Adam's lascivious glances (IX, 1015), Milton stresses the change in Eve from her newly created state in Book IV; through her choices, she has become herself lascivious and carnal.

Similarly, as Adam and Eve begin their labors in the Garden, Milton notes that among their activities, they "led the Vine/To wed her Elm" (*PL*, V, 215-216). As an image of fertility and mutual harmony, the marriage of the Elm and the Vine defines the perfect relationship which exists between Adam and Eve. Yet later, Eve urges that she and Adam separate and carry out their respective tasks alone,

> whether to wind
> The Woodbine round this Arbor, or direct
> The clasping Ivy where to climb...,
>
> (*PL*, IX, 215-217)

and in doing so she conflates the earlier use of the Elm and the Vine with a second *topos*, the Tree and the Ivy. By using the image as an argument for isolation, Milton suggests that these images, too, have secondary, destructive meanings and may refer not only to ideal marriage but also to entangling, destructive, and barren relationships. Milton thus shows, as he had through the use of *wanton*, that the perfection of Adam and Eve in Eden is not absolute and unchanging. Even desirable qualities and relationships are capable of changing through false choice, of impeding rather than enhancing human happiness.

Adam and Eve, then, are not static in Eden, not predeterminedly, unalterably perfect, but instead capable of growing toward a potential perfection. The initial sufficiency with which Adam and Eve are created is conditional and contingent, requiring constant vigilance to control and maintain. Adam and Eve are endowed with the consciousness and knowledge necessary to preserve their innocent state. They are able—and eminently free—to choose counter to that knowledge, however, and to allow passions to control them and direct them away from the will of God.

iii. The Fall

The Fall of Man in *Paradise Lost* is neither necessitated nor arbitrarily imposed. Adam and Eve make increasingly difficult choices, until finally the human pair is confronted by alternatives which become pivotal in their progress. Almost every act preceding the Fall foreshadows the decisions which must be made and the consequences should Adam and Eve choose falsely.

Eve's dream is one of the most important adumbrations of the Fall. John S. Diekhoff suggests that the dream in fact presages the situation and arguments of the Temptation and Fall, but denies the speculations of Tillyard, Waldock, Stein, Patrides, and others that it reveals an incipient tendency to evil in Eve. After all, in *Paradise Regained*,

> Satan disturbs Jesus's sleep with "ugly dreams" (*PR*, IV, 408). What they are is unspecified, but we do not conclude from his ugly dreams that there is an ugly streak in Jesus. The ugly dreams sprang not from Jesus's ethos, but from Satan's. So does Eve's dream. It was Satan, not Eve, who had fallen.[111]

Far from indicating an evil already present if as yet unexpressed, Eve's dream instead confirms her basic purity.

---

[111] John S. Diekhoff, "Eve's Dream and the Paradox of Fallible Perfection," MQ IV, (March 1970), pp. 5-6.

When Adam awakens from sleep, he sees the sleeping Eve, with her "Tresses discompos'd, and glowing Cheeks/As through unquiet rest" (*PL*, V, 101). The sense of disquiet and disorder seems ominous, particularly in light of undreamed temptations to be encountered in Book IX, when Milton purposely repeats the image of unhealthily glowing cheeks (886-887). This later repetition of *glow'd* looks back to the description of Eve after her premonitory dream and also contrasts with Adam's response to Eve's disobedience (IX 888-894), but neither Milton nor Adam blames Eve directly for the earlier disorder. Adam's comment, in fact, is quite the opposite: Eve's dream may be evil, but she is not (V, 96-100). Even assuming that the dream stemmed from Eve's Fancy "misjoining shapes" of previous conversations, Adam remains confident that any evil, if unapproved, will not remain.

Prior to the creation of Eve, Adam had had two dreams. In the first, the Creator had appeared to Adam, hailed him "First Father," and led him into the "Garden of Bliss." Upon awakening, Adam discovered that the dream had presaged reality. He stood in Eden and was soon after visited by the Creator. During the second dream, Adam had viewed the creation of Eve, including the important fact that she was formed "Flesh of [his] Flesh, Bone of [his] Bone." Again, upon awakening, Adam found that the dream was true. Consequently, Adam understands experientially that dreams are a valid mode of instruction and dissemination of knowledge. Eve's dream, then, becomes potentially important as a warning of possible alternative—and disobedient—actions. Significantly, both Adam and Eve are appalled by the dream and its implications. Adam concludes that a rejected evil cannot stain Eve's mind and draws a monitory hope from the unsettling experience:

> Evil into the mind of God or Man
> May come and go, so unapprov'd, and leave
> No spot or blame behind: Which gives me hope
> That what in sleep thou didst abhor to dream,
> Waking thou never wilt consent to do.
>
> (*P.L.*, V, 117-121)

Eve's dream, then, far from displaying inherent impulses toward sin in her subconscious, offers Milton an additional opportunity to show our First Parents confronting a situation which demands a choice—to approve or reject the content and implications of the dream. As in previous trials, both Adam and Eve decide correctly, abhor the dream, and look upon it as an admonition to zealous obedience.

The separation of Adam and Eve prior to Eve's temptation is even more closely related than Eve's premonitory dream to the decisions soon to be demanded of the human pair. One reading of the poem interprets the separation as in some sense a Fall itself, a consciously wrong decision entered into by Adam and sustained by Eve. Interpretations of the separation which imply that Adam and Eve are somehow fallen prior to their partaking of the fruit negate the essential freedom of Adam, Eve, or both, however, by either absolving humankind entirely from any real guilt or emphasizing the guilt of one party over that of the other. In addition, interpretations which view the separation as a Fall fail to note that the only commandment which Adam and Eve *could* break, simply because it was the only interdiction given them, was not to partake of the forbidden fruit. Before actually plucking and eating the fruit itself, their choices could not constitute the "First Disobedience" of Milton's theodicy, but merely could restrict the range of subsequent alternatives.

As Adam and Eve arrive at the close of their discussion of the proper husbanding for the Garden, Adam speaks directly to the central issue:

> But God left free the Will, for what obeys
> Reason, is free, and Reason he made right,
> But bid her well beware, and still erect,
> Lest by some fair appearing good surpris'd
> She dictate false, and misinform the Will
> To do what God expressly hath forbid.
> (*PL*, IX, 351-356)

Adam quite rightly perceives the real danger that the Will, which is created free and must remain free, may be at the mercy of the Reason. If Reason is perverted, the freedom of the Will becomes illusory and leads not to unhampered liberty of choice but to bondage. He simultaneously recognizes, however, both the Father's commitment to freedom in the universe and Eve's already proven facility in choosing correctly. His final words are monitory, while still acknowledging Eve's strength:

> Seek not temptation then, which to avoid
> Were better, and most likely if from mee
> Thou sever not: Trial will come unsought,
> Wouldst thou approve thy constancy, approve
> First thy obedience; th'other who can know,
> Not seeing thee attempted, who attest?
> But if thou think, trial unsought may find
> Us both securer than thus warn'd thou seem'st,
> Go; for thy stay, not free, absents thee more;
> Go in thy native innocence, rely
> On what thou hast of virtue, summon all,
> For God towards thee hath done his part, do thine.
>
> (*PL*, IX, 364-375)

There is no hint in Adam's words that Eve is unable to stand firmly or that he is allowing her an undue amount of freedom, nor do such hints appear in the narrative links between Adam's farewell and Eve's departure. Only as Eve fades from sight does the narrator reveal a foreknowledge of subsequent events (IX, 404-411).

Both Adam and Eve are thus to be exonerated of guilt in the separation scene. Both act according to their freedom to evaluate a situation, make decisions, and act on them. Adam has fulfilled his responsibility to Eve by counseling, advising, and finally warning, just as the Father (through Raphael) has counseled, advised, and warned Adam. Nor is Eve culpable. She is indeed sufficient to stand, having proved herself so by her conscious withdrawing from the image in the water and her abhorrence at the earlier dream. She is incomplete without Adam, just as he is incomplete without her, but neither is thereby inherently evil. Just as she received the prime Commandment from Adam's lips, so now she receives from him his permission to venture forth alone.

During the confrontation between Eve and the Serpent in the bower of roses, Satan as Serpent attempts to repeat the pattern of deceit and temptation which had served him so well in Heaven. His first words to Eve are digressive. He speaks not about the Tree, nor about the Commandment to abstain from its fruit, but rather about Eve as "sovran Mistress" and "A Goddess among Gods" (*PL*, IX, 547-548). Like Satan's first address to the rebel angels, this speech contains more than a grain of truth. Eve is indeed "ador'd and serv'd" by the Angels; in her surprise at hearing the brute speak, however, she fails to note that truth. Eve could have rejected any further temptation simply by reaffirming her relationship with God, just as could the rebel angels; but like the rebels, she allows herself to be diverted from the truth.

When Eve asks about the source of the Serpent's reason and speech, Satan describes the tree and the apples, and refers to the nature of his reason and understanding, now turned to "Speculations high or deep." Having partaken of the fruit, he contends, he,

> with capacious mind
> Consider'd all things visible in Heav'n,
> Or Earth, or Middle, all things fair and good....
> (*PL*, IX, 603-605)

Then, lest Eve catch him in his deceit and notice the disparity between his putative abilities and her own true ones—that is, between his dependence upon speculation and her right to know through revelation and right reason (aided by Adam) and to converse directly with celestial beings—Satan again diverts her with flattery, hailing her as "Sovran of Creatures, universal Dame" (IX, 612). There is more here than merely a play on Eve's vanity and pride. Satan knows of Eve's strength and power of choice. He equally knows that she has repeatedly repudiated false choice and confirmed her dedication to the will of Heaven. He thus begins his speech with half-truths—Eve is, after all, "Sovran of Creatures" in her role as helpmeet to Adam, just as she is the "Universal Dame," the only woman—before shifting rapidly to a personal and flattering appeal.

"Amazed"—in multiple and intentional senses of the word—by the Serpent's message, Eve chooses to accompany him to the tree. Regardless of Satan's specious logic and subversive rhetoric, however, she is still capable of righteous judgment, as her immediate reaction to the tree indicates:

> Serpent, we might have spar'd our coming hither,
> Fruitless to mee, though Fruit be here to excess,
> The credit of whose virtue rest with thee,
> Wondrous indeed, if cause of such effects.
> But of this Tree we may not taste nor touch;
> God so commanded, and left that Command
> Sole Daughter of his voice; the rest, we live
> Law unto ourselves, our Reason is our Law.
> (*PL*, IX, 647-654)

Like Abdiel, Eve consciously upholds the commandment of the Father, even questioning momentarily the truth of the Serpent's claims: "*if* cause of such effects." She chooses, however, to debate with the Serpent, which is precisely what he desires. Eve allows herself to be turned from revelation and reason to speculation and empty rhetoric. And, like the fallen angels whose errors she is retracing, she accepts Satan's challenge to argue on his own grounds, not on those with which she is experienced.

From this point, Eve's choices systematically limit her alternatives. Satan's appeal to her vanity becomes more overt as she accepts his words unhesitatingly as truth. As hunger urges her to eat, she rationalizes her desires through speculative philosophy, until, like the philosophizing demons in Pandemonium, she finds herself in "wand'ring mazes lost." She rejects as false what she knows to be true, that God does not forbid goodness and wisdom. With subtle and appropriate aids from Satan, she has argued herself into precisely the same state of mind as had the fallen angels. Secure in her supposed self-sufficiency and in the righteousness of her own reasoning, she partakes of the fruit.

His goal accomplished, Satan slinks unobserved into the thickets, while Eve, now disobedient and fallen, gorges herself intemperately on the Fruit, "Intent now wholly on her taste." She has allowed physical appetites and hollow intellectualizing to lead her to a decision, and then, for the first time, she chooses improperly. Evil ceases to be potential and intellectually perceived, and becomes experiential.

Having partaken and fallen, Eve becomes in turn a tempter. Her first reaction upon surfeiting herself with the fruit parallels Satan's desire for sovereignty and revenge (*PL*, IX, 124-134). She needs to destroy, to make others as she is herself. She wants to give Adam the illusion of freedom, while actually subordinating him to herself. She debates whether to incite him to partake or to keep him ignorant of her new status

> And render me more equal, and perhaps,
> A thing not undesirable, sometime
> Superior; for inferior who is free?
>
> (*PL*, IX, 823-825),

forgetting that acknowledging God's absolute superiority over all of creation, and hence the implicit rightness of his commandment, constitutes ultimate freedom. Following the pattern of disobedience first established by Satan and the rebel angels, Eve mistakes license for liberty. At the moment when she is celebrating her seemingly unbounded freedom, she has inextricably bound herself by the limitations and consequences of her sin.

During Eve's temptation and fall, Adam has been working in the Garden, plaiting a garland of roses for her. When Eve returns, she relates her experiences in a speech noticeably lacking in the epithetic and honorific addresses which had earlier invariably opened their dialogues. Her cheeks again glow, as on the morning following her dream; this time, however, the glow is self-induced and internal. Adam initially feels repulsed by her admission of disobedience (*PK*, IX, 888-891). In empathy with Earth and wounded Nature, the floral garland drops fading and unheeded to the ground.

This is Adam's opportunity. He has the power to judge righteously in his world (*PL*, VIII, 448). He may govern according to one of two patterns of actions: that of the Son, the true model; or that of

Satan, the rebel. There is no third alternative, since at this point, Adam must decide either for obedience or disobedience: he must refrain from eating as he had been commanded, or he must eat.

Adam is free to choose the pattern of the Son but he rejects this alternative, allowing the argument to shift instead from the essential question of obedience to the peripheral consideration of remaining with Eve or living alone in the Garden. Resolving to die with Eve, he submits to the bondage of disobedience and death as she had done. Adam willfully rejects true reason for false reasoning and rationalization, as had Satan, the demons, and Eve before him. He recapitulates in essence the arguments of the rebel chieftains in Pandemonium: perhaps the fruit is tainted by the Serpent and God will not notice that we have partaken; perhaps we shall indeed become as Gods; God will certainly not uncreate that which he has created, so death is impossible. Finally, in a phrase which echoes Satan's renunciation of good for evil, Adam consciously embraces death:

> ...if Death
> Consort with thee [Eve], Death is to mee as Life....
> ...to lose thee were to lose myself.
> (*PL*, IX, 953-954, 959)

As he withdraws from the path of righteousness, Adam, like Satan and Eve, ceases to judge clearly. His reason is so subverted by passions and speculations that he rejects what he knows to be true and accepts instead an inversion of universal law. Life, which is from God, is for him Death; and Death, which is of Satan alone, is his life.

Adam's choice is not forced upon him. Eve has fallen, but Adam need not, depending upon the strength of his faith. As he makes choices, however, he accepts the same non-logic and unreason which brought about the fall of one-third of the Heavenly Hosts. He makes his final choices against a backdrop of rationalizations and false premises, but he nonetheless makes them consciously (*PL.* IX, 996-999). Adam and Eve both choose the model provided by Satan. They abandon their true powers of choice through obedience and instead accept pride, distrust of the proven powers and wise purposes of the Deity, self-aggrandizement, self-delusion, and ultimate bondage to the consequences of their sin.

iv. *After the Fall*

The consequences of the Fall are immediate and obvious. Adam and Eve first experience guilty passion, awaken in shame, and discover their moral and physical nakedness. Even deeper, however, and more important, they lose any true understanding of their situation and perception of how best to repay their fault. Fallen humanity is no longer "sufficient to stand."

They clearly illustrate their inability to perceive events correctly when they attempt to shift the responsibility for their new state onto each other. Adam accuses Eve of failure to heed his warnings (IX, 1134-1139), while Eve, not to be out-argued, responds with a scathing condemnation of Adam, accusing him of failure to accept his responsibilities as her head (IX, 1155-1161). They berate each other for urging or allowing separation, apparently assuming that if Eve had not been present and alone in the bower at just the proper moment, the Fall would not have occurred. In reality, of course, they are simply side-stepping the issue. They are satisfied to conclude that the Fall was pre-determined as soon as they separated, not when they partook of the fruit.[112] Such an interpretation of events forces them to shift the blame for the earlier choice and for their present plight to one another.

The most serious and lasting result of the Fall, however, is their loss of a sense of rightful place in the universe and of their former ability to determine their own destiny through proper choice. As the debate in the closing lines of Book IX clearly indicates, Adam and Eve are unaware of the nature of their Fall; much less do they know how their sin might best be repaired.

Up to this point, the human pair has exactly paralleled Satan and his Crew. In each instance, individual rebellion and fall was brought about, not by external forces, but as the irrevocable results of

---

[112]Stella Revard, "Eve and the Doctrine of Responsibility," *PMLA* LXXXVIII, 1 (January 1973), p. 70.

choices freely entered into. Satan, the fallen angels, Eve, and Adam each knew the proper course of action and yet chose to diverge from that course to pride, selfishness, egoism, and willfulness. They desired freedom uninhibited by the superior will of the Deity; paradoxically, by seeking that illusory freedom they more completely destroyed the true freedom of obedience.

At this point, however, Adam and Eve introduce an anomaly. During the Divine Council in Book III, the Father indicates a significant difference between the relative falls of angels and man:

> The first sort by thir own suggestion fell,
> Self-tempted, self-deprav'd: Man falls deceiv'd
> By th' other first: Man therefore shall find grace,
> The other none: in Mercy and Justice both,
> Through Heav'n and Earth, so shall my glory excel,
> But Mercy first and last shall brightest shine.
>
> (*PL*, III, 129-134)

The mercy which the Father decrees for recalcitrant man allows Adam and Eve one final opportunity to assume responsibility for their sin, an opportunity denied to the fallen angels, through which Adam and Eve break the pattern of sin and return to obedience.

In Book X, the Father sends the Son to judge and sentence the transgressors. Christ asks the sinning pair

> how is [my voice] now become
> So dreadful to thee? that thou art naked, who
> Hath told thee? hast thou eaten of the Tree
> Whereof I gave thee charge thou shouldst not eat?
>
> (*PL*, X, 120-124)

The Son of course knows the answers to the questions, which are in fact a test of Adam's and Eve's willingness to admit their respective guilt. Adam in part fails when he attempts to thrust blame upon Eve, to which the Son responds:

> Was shee thy God, that her thou didst obey

> Before his voice, or was shee made thy guide,
> Superior, or but equal, that to her
> Thou didst resign thy Manhood, and the Place
> Wherein God set thee above her made of thee....
>
> *(PL,* X, 145-149)

Yet finally, Adam and Eve each admit their individual responsibility for transgression: "...and I did eat."

The Son fulfills the demands of justice, decreeing punishment and ultimate death for Adam and Eve, then softens the doom with mercy, symbolically clothing the human pair, hiding both the external and internal nakedness they have recognized (*PL,* IX, 220-223). The capacity to make wrong choices is necessary to the capacity to make any choices. Potential fallibility is an integral part of Adam's and Eve's perfection before the Fall. Part of what is restored to them after the Fall is the ability to return to making proper choices. As the Father decrees, "I will renew/His lapsed powers" (*PL,* III, 175-176). With the inward and outward clothing of the fallen pair, the Son makes possible a regeneration of choice in them, a restoration initiated when Adam and Eve not only recognize their individual guilt but seek to subsume the guilt of the other (*PL,* X, 831-834, 930-936). Thus for Adam and Eve alone, a fall from obedience and righteousness results in renewed opportunities to choose properly.

Having accepted the consequences of their sin, Adam and Eve perform that one act from which the fallen angels are perpetually excluded. They voluntarily return to the place of their judgment by the Son and

>   prostrate fell
> Before him reverent, and both confess'd
> Humbly thir faults, and pardon begg'd, with tears
> Watering the ground, and with thir sighs the Air
> Frequenting, sent from hearts contrite, in sign
> Of sorrow unfeign'd, and humiliation meek.
>
> *(PL,* X, 1099-1104)

Through their desire to repent, Adam and Eve make possible their ultimate restoration through the Son. In Raphael's words, through "long obedience tri'd," earth may be united with Heaven,

> And Earth be chang'd to Heav'n, and Heav'n to Earth,
> One Kingdom, Joy and Union without end.
> (*PL*, VII, 160-161)

CHAPTER SEVEN

Man's Freedom of Choice and the Return to God

> Philipp. ii. 12, c13: *work out your own salvation with fear and trembling. For it is God who works in you to will and act for his pleasure.* What can this mean but that God gives us the power to act freely, which we have not been able to do since the fall unless called and restored? We cannot be given the gift of will unless we are also given the freedom of action, because that is what free will means.
> —*The Christian Doctrine*, I, xvii

i. Fallen Man in a Fallen World

In the closing lines of *Paradise Lost*, Adam and Eve leave Eden and enter the fallen world their choices have created for them (*PL*, XII, 641-649). They have changed immensely since their Fall. Through the mercy and grace bestowed by the Father, they have entered upon the path to regeneration and restoration. They had once relinquished true choice for false reasoning and passion; now they are restored to at least partial freedom of choice. Having earlier voluntarily broken the bond between themselves by releasing each other's hand (IX, 385-386), they are now reunited.

Throughout *Paradise Lost*, Milton uses hands to define the ideal relationship between Adam and Eve and its subsequent perversion.

As the reader first beholds the human pair, they are joined in a perfect unity, "hand in hand" (IV, 319-324). Later, as Eve urges separation, Adam suggests that unity is more important than anything else: "our joint hands/Will keep [the Garden] from Wilderness with ease…" (IX, 244-245). Within a few lines, however, this sanguine hope is destroyed as Eve initiates the first breaking of the unity that man has thus far enjoyed. Milton describes Eve's departure into the isolation of the Garden in terms of hands: "from her husband's hand her hand/Soft she withdrew..." (IX, 385-386). From this point on, references to hands relate exclusively to individual—and often archetypally selfish—actions (IX, 780, 850-851, 888-895, 997). Finally, in a complete antithesis of their original and innocent unity, Adam is inflamed with Eve's beauty and provocativeness: "Her hand he seiz'd, and to a shady bank,/...He led her nothing loath..." (IX, 1037, 1039). Within this bower they experience the shame of passion and of marital disunity.

It is thus significant and essential to the purposes of the epic that Milton conclude not only with the visions of futurity, including the coming of the Savior, but also with an indication of the reunification of Adam and Eve. This he achieves by repeating almost verbatim his first image of ideal unity. The phrase "hand in hand" in Book XII, 648, occurs in precisely the same position as it had in Book IV, 321: "So hand in hand they passed...." The context of the later passage is quite different from that of the earlier, however, and in the differences between the two lies much of the meaning of *Paradise Lost*

In leaving Eden, the human pair weeps as they had wept at the end of Book X, but their tears are quickly wiped as they enter their new world. The first half of the final passage in the poem expresses the loss and suffering which accompanied the Fall; the last half is suffused with hope in the future and in the promises revealed to Adam. Fallen man in the fallen world is not to be left solely to his own devices: "and Providence thir guide."

As Adam and Eve take their "solitary way" from Eden into the world, they must begin to participate in the new experiences of choice that all must in future undergo. In Eden, all had been provided for them; in this new world, they alone must "choose/Thir place of rest." The visions with which Adam is armed as he leaves the Garden prepare him to choose correctly from among the limited options now open to him.

Adam had earlier hovered on the edge of an awareness of new options and responsibilities when he had cried out:

> O goodness infinite, goodness immense!
> That all this good of evil shall produce,
> And evil turn to good; more wonderful
> Than that which by creation first brought forth
> Light out of darkness! full of doubt I stand,
> Whether I should repent me now of sin
> By mee done and occasion'd, or rejoice
> Much more, that much more good thereof shall spring....
>
> (*PL*, XII, 469-476)

Through their choices Adam and Eve brought about the Fall of Man, but more importantly, they have come to a greater knowledge of their own potential than they had in their prelapsarian state. Like the rebel angels, Adam and Eve had fallen through their own choices. Unlike the rebels, however, Adam and Eve have experienced repentance, whereby regenerate humanity may turn from sin to God. Radzinowicz correctly assesses the importance of repentance for Adam and Eve when she states that the Fortunate Fall is such not merely because from evil God will return good, but also because humanity now knows that it is possible to combat evil and be victorious within, if only the will is strong enough. Adam and Eve have made two critical discoveries: first, that they must accept all responsibility for their decisions; and second, that it is possible to reverse the consequences of false choices. Repentance requires, in fact, that man "redeem his mistakes…through remaking the decisions which caused them. Each must break the pattern of mischoice in fresh choice."[113] Adam's discovery of these points is pertinent to him, to the poet, and to the reader, because it shows that Adam's posterity likewise will enjoy the freedom to make false choices and enslave

---

[113] Radzinowicz, "Eve and Dalila," pp. 157-158.

themselves to self and sin; or to choose correctly and by doing so regain a closeness to God and His intentions for them.

Before being sent forth from Eden "sorrowing, yet in peace," Adam and Eve had been given a preview of the world in which they and their posterity would live. Adam, and through him all humanity, would be given "many days" of grace,

> wherein thou *mayst* repent,
> And one bad act with many deeds well done
> *May'st* cover: well *may* then thy Lord appeas'd
> Redeem thee quite from Death's rapacious claim....
> (*PL*, XI, 255-258: italics mine)

Like Raphael's *may* in Book V (493), Michael's here suggests the varied possibilities for choice and restoration which Adam and Eve will share with their progeny. Michael's express purpose in visiting Adam and Eve is to show Adam "what shall come in future days," to show them the patterns of righteous and false choice which the sons and daughters of Adam will follow.

As the vision begins, Michael reveals the first effects of disobedience upon Adam's seed,

> who never touched
> Th'excepted Tree, nor yet with the Snake conspir'd,
> Nor sinn'd thy sin, yet from that sin derive
> Corruption to bring forth more violent deeds.
> (*PL*, XI, 425-428)

Adam beholds the murder of brother by brother, the first instance of physical Death among humankind. Adam is repelled by the sight but further horrified by Michael's subsequent revelation of the many forms which death will take, the foremost of which is intemperance, the earthly parallel to Eve's "inabstinence" in Paradise. To Adam's astonished question,

> Why should not Man,
> Retain still Divine similitude

> In part, from such deformities be free,
> And for his Maker's Image sake exempt?
>
> (*PL*, XI, 511-514)

Michael answers that subsequent humanity will choose freely to burden itself with "inhuman pains."

> Thir Maker's Image...then
> Forsook them, when themselves they vilifi'd
> To serve ungovern'd appetite, and took
> His Image whom they served, a brutish vice,
> Inductive mainly to the sin of *Eve*.
> Therefore so abject is their punishment,
> Disfiguring not God's likeness, but thir own,
> Or if his likeness, by themselves defac't
> While they pervert pure Nature's healthful rules
> To loathsome sickness, worthily, since they God's
> Image did not reverence in themselves.
>
> (*PL*, XI, 515-525)

Michael states explicitly that the punishments humanity will suffer through intemperance, like Satan's punishment in being forced to assume the form of the Serpent in Book X, are the direct result of conscious choice, of willing acceptance of the false pattern of action provided by Eve. Adam's response to the vision, "I yield it just... and submit" (XI, 526), is itself a reminder of how completely Adam's repentance has altered his view of matters since his fall in Book IX.

Next, Adam beholds a "spacious Plain," whose peaceful appearance disguises the wickedness and lasciviousness of its inhabitants, followed by a "wide Territory" of towns and cities ravaged by warfare and pillage. In the midst of the scene,

> one rising, eminent
> In wise deport, spake much of Right and Wrong,
> Of Justice, of Religion, Truth and Peace,
> And Judgment from above: him old and young

> Exploded, and had seiz'd with violent hands,
> Had not a Cloud descending snatch'd him thence
> Unseen amid the throng....
>
> *(PL,* XI, 665-671)

Adam is confounded by the prospect, not only of men dealing death "inhumanly to men" and multiplying "ten thousandfold the sin of him who slew/His Brother" (XI, 678-679), but also of humankind's willfully disregarding the warning of one who preaches repentance and judgment. Adam's vision of Enoch affords him, on the other hand, the first great example of proper choice within mortality and its concomitant rewards. Because of his unparalleled righteousness, Enoch is caught up directly into Heaven,

> to walk with God
> High in Salvation and the Climes of bliss,
> Exempt from Death; to show thee what reward
> Awaits the good, the rest what punishment....
>
> *(PL,* XI, 707-710)

The vision then turns from the "brazen Throat of War" to licentious "jollity and games,/To luxury and riot...." In the midst of blatant unrighteousness, a prophet again emerges to urge the people back to proper choice. Noah's protestations and warnings fail to convince his fellowmen, however, who suffer the consequences of their choice to sin—death.

By this point in the vision, Adam almost despairs completely for his children, crying out against a foreknowledge of the future which brings only grief. Adam had hoped for peace and happiness among his progeny but beholds instead "Peace to corrupt no less than War to waste" (XII, 784). Michael argues, on the other hand, that such regression from righteousness is essential to preserve man's freedom of choice:

> ...Earth shall bear
> More than anough, that temperance may be tri'd:
> So all shall turn degenerate, all deprav'd,

> Justice and Temperance, Truth and Faith forgot;
> One Man except, the only Son of light
> In a dark Age, against example good,
> Against allurement, custom, and a World
> Offended; fearless of reproach and scorn,
> Or violence, hee of thir wicked ways
> Shall them admonish, and before them set
> The paths of righteousness....
> (*PL*, XI, 804-814)

Through Noah, humanity is given an opportunity to turn from false choices and embrace righteousness; failing to make good use of this opportunity, individuals release themselves to the destruction of the flood. Only Noah and his family survive to rejoice in "peace from God, and Cov'nant new" (XI, 877). Adam sees the rainbow and questions its meaning, to which question Michael responds:

> So willingly doth God remit his Ire,
> Though late repenting him of Man deprav'd,
> Griev'd at his heart, when looking down he saw
> The whole Earth fill'd with violence, and all flesh
> Corrupting each thir way; yet those remov'd,
> Such grace shall one just Man find in his sight,
> That he relents, not to blot out mankind,
> And makes Cov'nant never to destroy
> The Earth again by flood....
> (*PL*, XI, 885-893)

The righteous choice of one just man is sufficient to offset the perversions of multitudes. Through Noah's obedience to God's commandments, humanity receives a second start, and the Father promises that the elements of the universe shall now

> ...hold thir course, till fire purge all things new,
> Both Heav'n and Earth, wherein the just shall dwell.
> (*PL*, XI, 900-901)

As Book XII begins, Michael pauses "Betwixt the world destroy'd and the world restor'd," just as Adam is now caught up between the lost world of Eden and the future world of time and history. Adam can no longer see the visions opened to him, so Michael relates the history of the "second stock" preserved from the flood. After a time of peace, Michael notes, "one shall rise/Of proud ambitious heart" who will reject the pattern of righteous choice offered by Enoch and Noah.

Milton's account of Nimrod begins by noting that Nimrod's rebellion against God, much like Satan's, follows a "long time [of] peace.../Under paternal rule" (XII, 23-24). Nimrod, whose name means "rebel," strives to "arrogate Dominion undeserv'd/Over his Brethren..." (XII, 27-28). Withdrawing with his followers—his "crew"—Nimrod settles on a plain

> wherein a black bituminous gurge
> Boils out from under ground, the mouth of Hell;
> Of Brick, and of that stuff they cast to build
> A City and Tow'r, whose top may reach to Heav'n;
> And get themselves a name...
> Regardless whether good or evil fame.
> (*PL*, XII, 41-45, 47)

Nimrod, like Satan, founds his capital on the elements of Hell itself. Through his inordinate pride, Nimrod chooses not only to tyrannize his fellowmen but also to challenge God by building a "Tow'r, whose top may reach to Heav'n...." Motivated by a jealous regard for his own name and reputation, and fearful lest "far disperst/In foreign Lands thir memory be lost..." (XII, 45-46), Nimrod assumes pretensions of godhood. His consequent punishment, like Satan's in Book X, is both just and largely self-chosen; the Father confuses the language of men by which Nimrod's fame was to have spread upon the earth.

Adam severely criticizes Nimrod for aspiring "above his Brethren," and for assuming

> Authority usurp'd, from God not giv'n:

> He gave us only over Beast, Fish, Fowl
> Dominion absolute; that right we hold
> By his donation; but Man over men
> He made not Lord; such title to himself
> Reserving, human left from human free.
> <div align="right">(<i>PL</i>, XII, 66-71)</div>

Adam has experienced the consequences of unjust desires for superiority not granted to men. Eve, in offering Adam the fruit, had considered gaining mastery over her natural head. Beyond this, however, Adam also perceives the irrationality of Nimrod's attempt at tyranny, since, as Adam asks, how could man even eat or breathe at the heights Nimrod intends to scale?

Michael's answer is in effect a key to understanding much of Adam's vision of human history. While in the Garden, Adam and Eve had been constantly instructed in the proper use of free choice. Through Raphael, they had learned of the just choices of the Son, of the loyal angels, and particularly of Abdiel, as well as of the destructive choices of Satan and his crew. As individuals, they had also made choices, failing only once to select the proper alternative. But that one false choice had cost them the joys of Eden and had brought upon them the doom of death. In his repentant state, Adam cannot conceive that individuals forewarned of the consequences of false choice could so easily embrace sin. Michael, however, reminds Adam of one far-reaching consequence of Adam's sin, the concomitant loss of true liberty and its constant companion, true reason:

>   yet know withal,
> Since thy original lapse, true Liberty
> Is lost, which always with right Reason dwells
> Twinn'd, and from her hath no dividual being;
> Reason in man obscur'd, or not obey'd,
> Immediately inordinate desires
> And upstart Passions catch the Government
> From Reason, and to servitude reduce
> Man till then free. Therefore since hee permits
> Within himself unworthy Powers to reign

> Over free Reason, God in Judgment just
> Subjects him from without to violent Lords;
> Who oft as undeservedly enthrall
> His outward freedom: Tyranny must be,
> Though to the Tyrant thereby no excuse.
>
> (*PL*, XII, 82-96)

Michael is quite clear in his denunciation of false choices; Adam's sin had weakened and obscured reason, yet the individual nonetheless permits his own passions to destroy his freedom, both internally and (through the tyranny of such men as Nimrod) externally.

In order that Adam find no excuse to blame God for limiting man's ability to reason and choose, Michael proceeds to discuss those who preserve their freedom, even in the face of sin. Abraham, Isaac, Israel, and Moses all provide examples of righteous choice, examples which all too few will follow. Even more importantly, through the promises made to Abraham and the "types and shadows" by which Moses instructs the children of Israel, mankind is made aware of the

> destin'd Seed to bruise
> The Serpent, by what mean he shall
> Achieve Mankind's deliverance
>
> (*PL*, XII, 233-235).

Adam is told that only as individuals accept the teachings and warnings of those prophets who foretell the coming Messiah can they draw nearer to the Father and regain the freedom they have lost; indeed, the Father will select one "peculiar Nation.../From the rest" and

> ...Laws and Rites
> Establisht, such delight hath God in Men
> Obedient to his will, that he voutsafes
> Among them to set up his Tabernacle,
> The holy One with mortal Men to dwell....
>
> (*PL*, XII, 244-248)

As a result of obedience, the Father restores in part the communications between Heaven and Earth that had existed unrestricted in Eden; the Holy One will sometimes descend to speak with men.

Michael does not thereby conclude, however, that humanity will long continue in such a state of blessed obedience:

> Doubt not but that sin
> Will reign among them, as of thee begot....
>
> ...they in thir earthly *Canaan* plac't
> Long time shall dwell and prosper, but...sins
> National interrupt thir peace,
> Provoking God to raise them enemies:
> From whom as oft he saves them penitent
> By Judges first, then under Kings....
>   (*PL*, XII, 285-286, 315-320)

Although Milton does not here identify the judges and kings individually, his treatment of choice and responsibility in *Samson Agonistes* largely clarifies the kinds of alternatives open to one man fully aware both of his fallen, mortal state and of his possibility for regeneration. Through Samson's encounters with the Chorus, Manoa, Dalila, Harapha, and the Officer, he learns experientially to choose correctly, and his choices awaken in him receptivity to the grace and divine illumination that he had once possessed and that he subsequently voluntarily relinquished through false choice. Samson, who at the beginning of the play had been associated with images of irrevocable spiritual darkness, is finally represented by images of light, flame, and the Phoenix:

> But he though blind of sight,
> Despis'd and thought extinguish't quite,
> With inward eyes illuminated
> His fiery virtue rous'd
> From under ashes into sudden flame....

> Like that self-begott'n bird
> In the *Arabian* wood embost,
> That no second knows nor third,
> And lay erewhile a Holocaust,
> From out her ashy womb now teem'd,
> Revives, reflourishes....
>
> (*SA* 1687-1691, 1699-1704)

As Samson moves through a series of choices, he doggedly eliminates all except those by which he could either fall to his earlier depths of despair (or lower) or rise through the power of regeneration. By overcoming the temptations presented by his visitants—the Chorus's temptation to despair, Manoa's temptation to ease, Dalila's temptation to uxoriousness, Harapha's temptation to egoistic heroism, and the Officer's temptation to resist the revealed will of God—Samson further submerges his own desires beneath those of God, while simultaneously providing for erring Israel a model of conscious, free, and proper choice and re-choice. If Samson does not literally deliver his people as a nation from the bondage of their enemies, he does provide a pattern by which they might individually orchestrate their deliverance from internal bondage to self and sin.

Michael does not, of course, refer directly to Samson in Book XII, but Milton's treatment of the later hero suggests the way in which he intends Michael's teachings to influence Adam. Enoch, Noah, Abraham, Moses, and—by inference in *Paradise Lost* and explicitly in *Samson Agonistes*—Samson each show the possibility of proper choice in the fallen world. Unlike the Father and the Son, the angels loyal and rebellious, and prelapsarian Adam and Eve, these prophets begin as fallen men. They have no absolute knowledge of God and of His plans for humanity; their awareness is dependent upon revelation and inspiration. They have received no patterns of obedience directly from Heavenly messengers, nor have they—in mortality—freely walked and talked with God, as Adam had in Eden. They are ultimately dependent upon faith, not knowledge. They are, in a word, mortal, and as such their experiences provide models with which all men may closely identify. Through false choice, the wicked—the scoffers of Noah's generation, Nimrod and his crew, the idolaters of Abraham's time—imprison themselves in sin, weaken their wills, and fall into damnation; through correct choices, those models pointed out by Michael show Adam that humanity might yet re-establish communication between Heaven and Earth and ultimately restore a proper relationship with God.

As Michael brings his revelation of human futurity to a close, he departs from the patterns of choice offered by men and returns to the divine pattern embodied in the God-man Christ, the Chosen Seed through whom the wound inflicted by the Serpent will be healed. Michael is quite clear, however, that the restoration offered by the "Anointed King Messiah" will avail only those who choose obedience to the will of Heaven. The Messiah comes to nullify Satan's "works/In thee [Adam] and in thy Seed"

> ...by fulfilling that which thou didst want,
> Obedience to the Law of God....
>
> So only can high Justice rest appaid.
> The Law of God exact he shall fulfill
> Both by obedience and by love, though love
> Alone fulfill the Law....
> (*PL*, XII, 396-397, 401-404)

Through Christ, the ransom required by Adam's sin will be paid. Man may then "the benefit embrace/By faith not void of works" (XII, 426-427) and as one whom the sacrifice of the Son shall redeem, undergo only a "death like sleep,/A gentle wafting to immortal Life" (XII, 434-435).

ii. The Destiny of Man

In the Miltonic universe, most creatures enjoy a stable existence; that is, there is little if any upward or downward movement, at least not since the rebellion of Satan and his crew. The Father and the Son are absolutes, with no need for change, while the angels determined their final status in the single choice of whether to remain true to the will of God or to follow Satan in rebellion. Once they had chosen a side, their choices became irrevocable; the loyal angels would not fall, and the rebels could not repent. Raphael suggests, of course, that the loyal angels, proceeding as they do from God, will ultimately "up to him return" (*PL*, V, 470) as they persevere in absolute righteousness. He seems to refer, however, to the loyal angels as a group, rather than to individuals. Only one level of creation in Milton's universe remains fluid. Humankind alone is capable of rising or falling according to individual, on-going choices. Man alone may rise to share in Godhood or fall to the level of the devils. Created in time and subject to error, man nevertheless is endowed with the potential for eternity.

Both Adam and Eve and the demons had freely fallen. As Milton strongly argued, however, there exists a vast difference between the Fall of Man and that of Satan and the rebels, as a result of which Satan is eternally damned, while humanity receives the mercy of possible restoration. Because Satan interfered with the progress of mankind, in the hope of corrupting man and winning him for himself and for Hell, the consequences of human sin are ameliorated by the gratuitous love and mercy of God, manifested in the sacrifice of the Son. Adam and Eve become aware of their sin and choose repentance and humble faith, thus preparing the way for God to bring to pass the highest good, the salvation and redemption of humanity. Through his efforts at destruction, Satan paradoxically achieves the opposite of his ends. Man is potentially able to achieve a level of existence higher than that which he now enjoys, or than he once enjoyed in Eden.[114] The choice to do so is largely his and is contingent upon his desire to walk uprightly and to be obedient.

---

[114] Diane McColley disagrees with this assertion, however. Citing Milton, she writes, "'The *restoration of Man* is that act whereby man, being delivered from sin and death by God the Father through Jesus Christ, is raised to a far more excellent state of grace and glory than that from which he had fallen. In this restoration are comprised the *redemption* and *renovation of man.*' Milton does *not* say 'a more excellent state...than if he had not fallen,' and since Adam and Eve are in the process of being raised by grace and merit before the Fall, we need not think their disobedience was fortunate or that the Son's participation need have been any less triumphant without it" (*Milton's Eve* [Urbana: University of Illinois Press, 1983], p. 136n.)

Milton was not alone in his endeavors to understand who man was and what he might become. Many of the early Church Fathers confronted directly the problem of man's nature and destiny. Origen, Lactantius, Basil, Tatian, and Theophilus all believed that man was potentially or actually higher than the angels; several argued explicitly that through grace and freedom of choice,

> man was given the means of advancement, in order that maturing and becoming perfect, and being even declared a god, he might ascend into heaven in possession of immortality. For man had been made a middle nature, neither wholly mortal, nor altogether immortal, but capable of either.[115]

Augustine's teachings on the destiny of man, however, predominated over other interpretations. He argued that man might rise only to angelic status. The *Enchiridion* notes that man (provided he keep his innocence) was to rise to better things than he then knew. Even more directly, in the *De Civitate Dei*, Augustine wrote:

> For God had not made man like the angels, in such a condition that, even though they had sinned, they could none the more die. He had made them, that if they discharged the obligations of obedience, an angelic immortality and a blessed eternity might ensue, without the intervention of death; but if they disobeyed, death should be visited on them with just sentence.[116]

After Augustine, the view that man was originally intended to share angelic status was widely accepted. With the rise of humanism during the Renaissance, however, the optimism surrounding man's nature and destiny increased appreciably. Neoplatonic philosophy

---

[115] Evans, pp. 78, 86; citing Theophilus. See also Lyon, p. 82; James Barker, p. 70; Eastland, p. 14; and Hartwell, p. 75.

[116] Evans, p. 93-94.

taught that through moral perfection, the body and soul would become purified and rarified, approaching the perfection which is God. Ficino, Pico, and others dwelt on man's potential godhood, ultimately concluding that "The Absolute is within us, and God became man in order that man might become God."[117]

Augustine had believed that only the Fall intervened between man and God's original intention to elevate him to angelic status. Milton denies this answer; as Milton portrays the immutable plan of God, the Father will create from the chaos and destruction inflicted by Satan a new order of existence higher than even that of the pre-existing angels.

Paradise Lost contains several suggestions as to the final disposition of humanity. The one most frequently discussed by critics occurs during Raphael's conversation with Adam, as the angelic visitor discourses on the underlying unity of all creation. Raphael speaks briefly of angelic eating and concludes with the statement that

> time may come when men
> With Angels may participate, and find
> No inconvenient Diet, nor too light Fare:
> And from these corporal nutriments perhaps
> Your bodies may at last turn all to spirit,
> Improv'd by tract of time, and wing'd ascend
> Ethereal, as wee, or may at choice,
> Here or in Heav'nly Paradises dwell....
> (*PL*, V, 493-500)

According to Curry, Milton here introduces a new doctrine of a force which is able to "overleap the bounds proportioned to its kind and attain a sphere to which it was not originally intended...." Since man, like the angels, is capable of "sublimating the fruit of trees to sensitive and animal spirits, thence to intellectual, whence the soul receives discursive reason," it follows that "in time the purified spirits of men may achieve the conversion of their crass bodies into an

---

[117] Roberts, p. 27.

ethereal substance like that which is formed into the bodies of angels."[118]

With very few exceptions, critics seem to assume that Raphael's conclusions are also those of God—and of Milton. The repetition of *may* in lines 493 and 497 apparently suggests the conditional nature of man's hopes; only through complete obedience and purification can man achieve the status the angels have enjoyed since their creation. Rarely is the suggestion made that *may* just as appropriately refers to Raphael's own doubts and ignorance. From experience and reason, he has drawn a personal conclusion about man's final potential.

Raphael is not the first, however, to speculate that man might eventually attain equality with the angels. During the Infernal Council, Satan had remarked that perhaps this new creature was to assume the places forfeited by the fallen angels. To the devils, man is

> A race of upstart Creatures, to supply
> Perhaps our vacant room....
>
> (*PL*, II, 83-835)

The fact that both Raphael (who does not explicitly claim divine approval for his speculations) and Satan (who was not present during the creation of man and hence has no way of knowing the Father's true motives) agree in anticipating man's elevation to angelic status renders the suggestion somewhat suspect. Just prior to the fall of Adam and Eve, Satan reiterates his claim that the Father is

> Determin'd to advance into our room
> A Creature form'd of Earth, and him endow,
> Exalted from so base original,
> With Heav'nly spoils, our spoils....
>
> (*PL*, IX, 148-151)

---

[118] Curry, p. 170.

According to Raphael and Satan, man is to become heir to the glories relinquished by the fallen angels.

Critics generally accept Raphael's explanation of man's destiny, apparently unaware that there is another possibility offered. As Satan speaks to Eve in the Garden, he urges her to partake of the fruit and thereby

> be as Gods,
> Knowing both Good and Evil as they know.
> That ye should be as Gods, since I as Man,
> Internal Man, is but proportion meed,
> I of brute human, yee of human Gods....
> And what are Gods that Man may not become
> As they, participating in God-like food?
> (*PL*, II, 708-711, 716-717)

Satan suggests to Eve that the fruit may be capable of making her equal not merely with Adam, but perhaps with the Father Himself. It is inviting to assume that Satan is simply appealing to Eve's vanity, and in part he is. It is equally important to remember, however, that much of what Satan says must be interpreted according to the circumstances surrounding him. When in Hell, he speaks as commanding General to defeated but valiant troops; when alone, as on Mount Niphates, he presumably vents his true feelings; and when in dialogue with Eve, he speaks whatever falsehoods or partial truths might best serve his purposes.

Ironically, much of what Satan includes in his seductive argumentation is in part truth, although only so from the Father's eternal perspective, not from Satan's limited and inverted view. When he urges knowledge through partaking of the fruit, for example, Satan is in fact urging Eve to make the decision by which she, and Adam after her, will enter mortality and thus fulfill the deeper purposes of the Father—to bring good out of evil. Thus Satan's apparent lie possibly has more truth in it than Raphael's apparent truth. Such a reversal would fit the paradoxical structure of anticipation and denial which forms the pattern of obedience in Milton's poetic universe.

There is, of course, at least one sense in which Milton suggests that the angels themselves are gods and that Raphael and Satan are thus correct in their speculations. As the Father announces the elevation of the Son, He speaks to the assembled angels:

> But all ye Gods,
> Adore him, who to compass all this dies,
> Adore the Son, and honor him as mee.
> (*PL*, III, 341-343)

If the angels are already in some way gods, then Raphael and Satan might legitimately speak of man as potentially a god. Milton is quite clear, however, that the ultimate union of the Angels with the Father, under their "Head Supreme" the Christ, is a different kind of union than that in which man might participate through the mediation of the redeeming Christ. There is ample evidence in *Paradise Lost* that Milton conceived of man as potentially superior to the angels.

In Book VII, he makes explicit the suggestion that man, as subsequent creation to the angels, must be superior to the angels, since God would not follow one creation by a lesser one. As Raphael recounts the creation of the earth, he states:

> There wanted yet the Master work, the end
> Of all yet done....
>
> ...grateful to acknowledge whence his good
> Descends, thither with heart and voice and eyes
> Directed in Devotion, to adore
> And worship God Supreme *who made him chief
> Of all his works....*
> (*PL*, VII, 505-506, 512-516; italics mine)

In addition, the idea that man is potentially one with God appears at least four times in *Paradise Lost*: once as the Father speaks in the Celestial Council; twice as Adam contemplates his state on earth; and once as Christ appeals to the Father on behalf of fallen man. As the Father praises the Son's decision to enter mortality, he says:

> because in thee
> Love hath abounded more than Glory abounds,
> Therefore thy Humiliation shall exalt
> With thee thy Manhood also to this Throne;
> Here shalt thou sit incarnate, here shalt reign
> Both God and Man, Son both of God and Man,
> Anointed universal King; all Power
> I give thee, reign forever, and assume
> Thy merits....
>
> (*PL*, III, 311-319)[119]

The Son is God and also Man; in him a link is created by which Man and God become as one, exalted through the Son to the Throne of God.

As Adam recounts his history in Book VIII, he includes a reference to the possibility of man's union with the Creator:

> Thou in thy secrecy although alone,
> Best with thyself accompanied, seek'st not
> Social communication, yet so pleas'd,
> Can'st raise thy Creature to what highth thou wilt
> Of Union or Communion....
>
> (*PL*, VIII, 427-431)

Later, as Eve urges him to disobedience, Adam recalls his earlier belief that man might indeed be elevated, to "Union or Communion" with God. This time, however, he loses sight of the all-important qualification that such elevation takes place only as man continues in strict obedience to God's will. Adam sees in the Fruit an opportunity to gain quickly that which the Father has promised only after long proof of obedience. The Fruit offers

---

[119] See also *PL*, III, 281-294, 303-304.

> Proportional ascent, which cannot be
> But to be Gods, or Angels Demi-gods.
>
> (*PL*, IX, 936-937)

The true "Union or Communion" which Adam had once understood includes not only the two natures present in Christ, not only Adam himself, but also all humanity, to the extent that they too acquiesce to the Father's purposes.

In Book XI, the Christ offers precisely this kind of union to all that are his offspring, that is, who adhere to him in faith and obedience:

>   let mee
> Interpret for [man], mee his Advocate
> And propitiation, all his works on mee
> Good or not good ingraft, my Merit those
> Shall perfet, and for these my Death shall pay.
> Accept me, and in mee from these receive
> The smell of peace toward Mankind, let him live
> Before thee reconcil'd, at least his days
> Number'd, though sad, till Death, his doom (which I
> To mitigate thus plead, not to reverse)
> To better life shall yield him, where with mee
> All my redeem'd may dwell in joy and bliss,
> *Made one with me as I with thee am one.*
>
> (*PL*, XI, 32-44; italics mine)

Christ offers humanity a second alternative—that through repentance and obedience they may be raised above the union existing between God and the loyal angels into a union with God through Christ. The Son speaks to the Father on man's behalf, and that plea is accepted. Man is to become one with the Deity Himself.

Christ pleads that "All my redeem'd" might be "Made one with me as I with thee am one." In *The Christian Doctrine*, Milton presents his evidence for a carefully restricted unity of the Father and the Son:

> Firstly, they are one in that they speak and act as one.... Christ distinguishes the Father from the whole of his own being. However, he does say that the Father dwells in him, though this does not mean that their essence is one, only that their communion is extremely close. Secondly, he declares that he and the Father are one in the same way as we are one with him: that is, not in essence, but in love, in communion, in charity, in spirit, and finally in glory.
>
> (*CD*, I, v, 220)

Further, while the "name, attributes, and works of God and the divine office itself" (*CD*, I, v, 223) are frequently shown by Trinitarians to be applied to both the Father and the Son, Milton demonstrates through logic and proof texts that the "attributes of divinity" relate exclusively to the Father (227). This fact notwithstanding, he subsequently argues that the Son receives "from the Father his individuality, his life itself, his attributes, his works, and, lastly, his divine honor" (259). And among the attributes of the Son which tie him to the Father are specifically defined manifestations of omnipresence, omniscience, authority, omnipotence, divine glory, and creation, the latter "not by him, but by the Father" through him (264-274). In the Son, each is secondary to the Father's power and glory but nonetheless indicates ways in which the Father and the Son are one.

Through the Father's *attribution* (Milton's term) of powers to the Son, the Son is uniquely capable of effecting the Restoration of man: "the act by which man, freed from sin and death by God the Father through Jesus Christ, is raised to a *far more excellent state of grace and glory than that from which he fell*" (*CD*, I, xiv, 415; italics mine). Or, as the poet states, only through the mediatory function of Christ can man "regain the blissful Seat" (*PL*, I, 4-5), with his "intellect...to a very large extent restored to its former state of enlightenment and the will...restored, in Christ, to its former freedom" (*CD*, I, xxi, 478). While the restoration of intellect may be in some way limited, the restoration of freedom is absolute.

Ultimately man may achieve "complete glorification," or an "eternal and utterly happy life, arising chiefly from the sight of God" (*CD*, I, xxxiii, 630), "accompanied by the renovation of, and our possession of, heaven and earth and all those creatures in both which might be useful or delightful to us" (632)

This is the *oneness* which man is invited to share, a oneness resulting from the relationship between man and God in terms of freedom, moral choice, the mediation of the Son, and even (as noted in Chapter V) the substance of which man's spirit and material body are created. Man is part of God; though fallen, he may yet be restored to his original promised birthright. He is declared co-heir to the love, communion, agreement, charity, spirit, and glory of Christ and thereby of God—contingent only upon man's free decision to walk in obedience to the laws of God.

EPILOGUE

Throughout his works, Milton constantly emphasizes the importance of man's moral freedom as one mode by which man may find his proper place among the rational beings inhabiting his universe. Milton himself, of course, amply illustrates his own thesis; whenever he confronts alternative interpretations of rational behavior—whether of human, infernal, or celestial beings—he carefully selects that possibility which most clearly requires freedom of choice. The various elements of Christian theology, philosophical speculation, and personal inference that make up Milton's world view fit together to suggest a universe in which independent choice extends from the Creator throughout all levels of rational creatures.

C. A. Patrides argues, for example, that Milton viewed history as essentially Christocentric and lineal—that is, as moving from the six days of creation to the final Judgment of mankind, with the figure of the incarnate God-man standing both inside and outside of time. Thus Milton is the final inheritor of a tradition extending from Eusebius to Augustine, thence to Jerome and Orosius, Isidore and Bede, Otto of Freising and Vincent of Beauvais, and finally to Dante and the Renaissance. As Christians, each was able to "see the origin of the world, and the end of the world, and the intervening time."[120]

Although Patrides's argument is strong, supported as it is by references to the prose and poetry, particularly *Paradise Lost*, Milton does not hesitate to include in what Patrides calls the Christian view of history a subtle borrowing from Greco-Roman cyclical theories.

---

[120] C. A. Patrides, *The Phoenix and the Ladder: The Rise and Decline of the Christian View of History* (Berkeley: University of California Press, 1964), pp. 6, 65-66

Milton's conception of freedom—the most important element in human, angelic, and perhaps even divine natures—is in a very important sense cyclical. Moral freedom begins with the Father, for whom freedom of choice is an absolute principle freely imparted to His creatures according to His will and decree. As fallen men make proper choices—guided by the positive example of the Son and the negative examples of Satan, of the angels who fell with him, and of the fallen and yet unrepentant Adam and Eve—their impaired and limited freedom is restored and leads them back to unity with God, their source. And as individuals make improper choices and thus consciously draw away from the goodness of the Father, He withdraws from them the right to continued choice; they have embraced enslavement, and that choice must be respected. Human history is then both linear and cyclical; humanity does indeed move through time, from a distinct beginning to a distinct end, yet through the choices made during mortality, individuals may be reunited with the Father, who is without beginning and end, and is outside of time. Humanity may, in short, return to their source.

Milton's treatment of freedom of choice in the Father, the Son, and material universe, the angels, and man is consistent with his visions and his purposes. His concern with moral choice is the key by which the reader may enter into and understand Milton's universe. Man's freedom of choice is the single human capacity by which universal harmony, once disturbed by conscious sin, may yet be restored and man able "at choice" in "Heav'nly Paradises" to dwell.

BIBLIOGRAPHY OF
WORKS CITED AND CONSULTED

Adams, Robert, ed. *The Circe of Signior Giovanni Battista Gelli of the Academy of Florence, Consisting of Ten Dialogues between Ulysses and several men transformed into beasts, satirically representing the various passions of mankind and the many infelicities of human life, Done out of Italian by Mr. Thomas Brown (of facetious memory)*. Ithaca, New York: Columbia University Press, 1963.

Allain, Mathé. "The Humanist's Dilemma: Milton, God, and Reason," *CE*, 27 (1966), 379-384.

Arnold, Marilyn. "Milton's Accessible God: The Role of the Son in *Paradise Lost*." *MQ*, VII, 3 (October, 1973), 65-72.

Augustine. *Admonition and Grace*. Ed. John Courtney Murray, in *The Fathers of the Church*, gen. ed. Roy Joseph Deferrari. New York: Fathers of the Church, Inc., 1947, IV, 239-309.

_____ . *Enchiridion [Faith, Hope, and Charity]*. Trans. Bernard M. Peebles in *The Fathers of the Church*, gen. ed. Roy Joseph Deferrari. New York: The Fathers of the Church, Inc., 1947, IV, 357-472.

_____ . *On Nature and Grace*, in *Saint Augustin's Anti-Pelagian Works*. Trans. Peter Holmes and Robert Ernest Wallace, in *A Select Library of the Nicene and Post-Nicene Fathers of the Christian Church*, ed. Philip Schaff. 1887; rpt. Grand Rapids, Michigan: William B. Eerdmans Publishing Company, 1956, V.

_____ . *On the Grace of Christ*, in *Saint Augustin's Anti-Pelagian Works*. Trans. Peter Holmes and Robert Ernest Wallace, in *A Select Library of the Nicene and Post-Nicene Fathers of the Christian Church*, ed. Philip Schaff. 1887; rpt. Grand Rapids, Michigan: William B. Eerdmans Publishing Company, 1956, V.

Backman, Milton V., Jr. *American Religions and the Rise of Mormonism*. Salt Lake City, Utah: Deseret Book Company, 1970.

Bainton, Roland H. "Man, God, and the Church in the Age of the Renaissance," in *The Renaissance: Six Essays*, ed. Walter K. Ferguson, et. al. New York: Harper Torchbooks, 1962, 77-96.

Baker, Herschel. *The Image of Man: A Study of the Idea of Human Dignity in Classical Antiquity, the Middle Ages, and the Renaissance*. 1947; rpt. New York: Harper Torchbooks, 1961.

Bangs, Carl Oliver. *Arminius*. Nashville: Abingdon Press, 1971.

Barker, Arthur E. *Milton and the Puritan Dilemma*. Toronto: University of Toronto Press, 1942

_____. "Structural and Doctrinal Pattern in Milton's Later Poems," in *Essays in English Literature from the Renaissance to the Victorian Age Presented to A. S. P. Woodhouse*. Ed. Millar MacLure and F. W. Watt. Toronto: University of Toronto Press, 1964, 169-194.

Barker, James L. *Apostasy from the Divine Church*. Private publication: Kate Montgomery Barker, 1960.

Bartholomew, Ruth. "Some Sources of Milton's Doctrine of Free Will." Diss. Western Reserve University, 1945.

Bowra, C. M. *From Virgil to Milton*. 1945; rpt. London: Macmillan, 1967.

Brisman, Leslie. *Milton's Poetry of Choice and Its Romantic Heirs*. Cornell University Press, 1973.

Cassirer, Ernst, Paul Oscar Kristeller, and John Herman Randall, Jr., eds. *The Renaissance Philosophy of Man*. 1948; rpt. Chicago: University of Chicago Press, 1971.

Complete Prose Works of John Milton, Vols. I-VIII. General Ed., Don M. Wolfe. New Haven: Yale University Press, 1953-1982.

Conklin, George Newton. *Biblical Criticism and Heresy in Milton*. New York: King's Crown Press, 1949.

Cudworth, Ralph. *The True Intellectual System of the Universe: The First Part; wherein ALL the REASON and PHILOSOPHY of*

ATHEISM is Confuted; and its IMPOSSIBILITY Demonstrated. 1678; rpt. Stuttgart-Bad Cannstatt: Friedrich Frommann Verlag, 1964.

Curry, Walter Clyde. *Milton's Ontology, Cosmogony, and Physics.* 1957; rpt. Lexington, Kentucky: University of Kentucky Press, 1966.

Diekhoff, John S. "Eve's Dream and the Paradox of Fallible Perfection." *MQ*, IV, 1 (March, 1970), 5-7.

Empson, William. "Milton's God," *Listener*, 64 (1960), 11-13.

Erasmus, Desiderius. *On Free Will*, trans. Ernst F. Winter. *Erasmus-Luther: Discourse on Free Will.* New York: Frederick Ungar Publishing Co., Inc., 1961

Evans, J. M. *Paradise Lost and the Genesis Tradition.* Oxford: Clarendon Press, 1968.

Ficino, Marcilio. "Five Questions Concerning the Mind," in Ernst Cassirer, and others, eds., *The Renaissance Philosophy of Man*, 1948; rpt. Chicago: University of Chicago Press, 1971.

Harrison, A. W. *Arminianism.* London: Duckworth, 1937.

Hartwell, Kathleen E. *Lactantius and Milton.* Cambridge, Massachusetts: Harvard University Press, 1929.

Hefele, Charles Joseph. *A History of the Councils of the Church from the Original Documents.* Trans. William B. Clark. 1895; rpt. New York: AMS Press, 1972, IV.

Hughes, Merritt Y. *John Milton: Complete Poems and Major Prose.* New York: Odyssey Press, 1957.

Huizinga, Johan. *Erasmus and the Age of Reformation.* New York: Harper Torchbooks, 1957.

Hunter, William B., Jr., C. A. Patrides, and J. H. Adamson. *Bright Essence: Studies in Milton's Theology.* Salt Lake City, Utah: The University of Utah Press, 1971.

Kelley, Maurice, ed. *CPW of John Milton, ca. 1658-ca. 1660: The Christian Doctrine.* Gen. ed. Don M. Wolfe. New Haven: Yale University Press, 1973, VI.

_____ . *This Great Argument: A Study of Milton's De Doctrina Christiana as a Gloss upon Paradise Lost.* Princeton: Princeton University Press, 1941.

Lawry, Jon S. "'Eager Thought': Dialectic in Lycidas," in *Milton: Modern Essays in Criticism*, ed. Arthur E. Barker. London: Oxford University Press, 1965, 112-124.

Le Comte, Edward S. "Areopagitica as a Scenario for *Paradise Lost*," in *Achievements of the Left Hand*, ed. Michael Lieb and John T. Shawcross. Amherst, Massachusetts: The University of Massachusetts Press, 1974, 121-141.

Lewalski, Barbara K. *Milton's Brief Epic: The Genre, Meaning, and Art of Paradise Regained*. Providence, Rhode Island: Brown University Press, 1966.

Lewis, C. S. *A Preface to Paradise Lost*. 1942; rpt. London: Oxford University Press, 1969.

Lyon, Edgar T. *Apostasy to Restoration*. Salt Lake City, Utah: Deseret Book Company, 1960.

_____. *The Poetry of Meditation: A Study in English Religious Literature of the Seventeenth Century*. New Haven: Yale University Press, 1954.

McColley, Diane Kelsey. "Free Will and Obedience in the Separation Scene of *Paradise Lost*." *SEL*, 12 (Winter, 1972), 103-120.

_____. *Milton's Eve*. Urbana: University of Illinois Press, 1983.

McDill, Joseph Moody. *Milton and the Pattern of Calvinism*. 1938; rpt. Folcroft, Pennsylvania: The Folcroft Press 1969.

Nicolson, Marjorie Hope. "Milton and the *Conjectura Cabbalistica*." *PQ*, vi, (January, 1 927), 1-18.

Panofsky, Erwin. *Hercules am Scheidewege und andere antike Bildstoffe in der neueren Kunst*. Leipzig: B. G. Teubner, 1930.

Parker, William Riley. *Milton: A Biography*. Oxford: Clarendon Press, 1968, I.

Patrick, John M. "Milton's Conception of Sin as Developed in *Paradise Lost*." Utah State University Monograph Series, VII, 5 (June, 1960).

Patrides, C. A. "An Open Letter on the Yale Edition of *De Doctrina Christiana*." *MQ*, VII, 3 (October, 1973), 72-74.

_____. *The Phoenix and the Ladder: The Rise and Decline of the Christian View of History*. University of California Publications English Studies, 29. Berkeley: University of California Press, 1964,

_____. "The Salvation of Satan," *JHI*, 28 (1967),467-478.

Pico, Giovanni, della Mirandola. *Oration on the Dignity of Man.* Trans. A. Robert Caponigri. Chicago: Henry Regnery Company, 1956.

Radzinowicz, Mary Ann Nevins. "Eve and Dalila: Renovation and the Hardening of the Heart," in *Reason and Imagination: Studies in the History of Ideas, 1660-1800.* Ed. J. A. Mazzeo. New York: Columbia University Press, 1962, 155-181.

Revard, Stella. "Eve and the Doctrine of Responsibility in *Paradise Lost.*" *PMLA*, LXXXVIII, 1 (January, 1973), 69-78.

Richmond, Hugh M. *The Christian Revolutionary: John Milton.* Berkeley: University of California Press, 1974.

Roberts, James D., Sr. *From Puritanism to Platonism in Seventeenth Century England* The Hague: Martinus Nijhoff, 1968.

Robins, Harry F. *If This Be Heresy: A Study of Milton and Origen.* Illinois Studies of Language and Literature, 51. Urbana, Illinois: University of Illinois Press, 1963.

Saurat, Denis. *Milton, Man and Thinker.* New York: The Dial Press, 1925.

Schaff, Philip, ed, *A Select Library of the Nicene and Post-Nicene Fathers of the Christian Church.* 1887; rpt. Grand Rapids, Michigan: William B. Eerdmans Publishing Company, 1956.

Seaman, John E. *The Moral Paradox of Paradise Lost.* The Hague: Mouton, 1971.

Sprott, S. E. "The Damned Crew." *PMLA*, LXXXIV, 3 (May, 1969), 492-500.

Steadman, John M. "The Causal Structure of the Fall." *JHI*, XXI (1960), 180-197.

_____. *Epic and Tragic Structure in Paradise Lost.* Chicago: The University of Chicago Press, 1976.

Stoll, Elmer Edgar. "Give the Devil His Due: A Reply to Mr. Lewis." *RES*, o.s. XX (1944), 108-124.

Tuve, Rosemond. *Images and Themes in Five Poems by Milton.* Cambridge, Massachusetts: Harvard. University Press, 1957.

Ulreich, John C. "'Sufficient to Have Stood': Adam's Responsibility in Book IX,." *MQ*, V, 2 (May, 1971), 38-42.

Valla, Lorenzo. *Dialogue on Free Will,* trans. Charles Edward Trinkaus, in *The Renaissance Philosophy of Man*, ed. Ernst Cassirer, Paul Oskar Kristeller, and John Herman Randall, Jr. 1948; rpt. Chicago: The University of Chicago Press, 1971.

Wallerstein, Ruth. *Richard Crashaw: A Study in Style and Poetic Development*. Madison, Wisconsin: University of Wisconsin Press, 1959.

Winter, Ernst F., trans. and ed. *Erasmus-Luther: Discourse on Free Will*. New York: Frederick Ungar Publishing Co., Inc., 1961.

INDEX

Abdiel (Angel): 107-108, 131-134, 140-142, 151, 168, 183
Abraham: 44-45, 184, 186, 187
Achilles, Achillean: 107, 142
Adams, Robert: 30n
Adamson, J. H.: 97
Aldhelm: 24
Alexander of Hales: 33
Andrewes, Lancelot: 38
Angelic eating: 125
Antitrinitarianism: 93, 96, 121
Apocatastasis: 147
Apollo: 26, 61
Apuleius: 128
Aquinas, Thomas: 16, 33
Arianism: 7, 93-96, 98
Aristotle, Aristotelian: 16, 25, 42, 81, 124
Arius (See Arianism)
Arles, Synod of (475 A.D.): 22
Arminius, Arminianism: 7, 15, 24n, 25, 35-37, 42
Arnold, Marilyn: 101n
Arthur, Arthurian: 37
Astraea: 37, 42, 49
Athanasius: 93-96
Atonement: 35-36, 98, 105
Augustine of Hippo: 16, 17-25, 32-34, 37, 42, 128, 189, 190, 198
    Admonition and Grace: 17, 18n, 19n
    De Civitate Dei: 189
    Enchiridion: 18n, 189
    On Nature and Grace: 19n
    On the Grace of Christ: 21, 22n

Avencebrol: 123
Avitus of Vienne: 24
Aylmer, John: 38, 42
Babb, Lawrence: 8
Bacchus: 55
Backman, Milton J., Jr.: 36n
Baker, Herschel: 8, 17, 30n, 31, 33n
Barker, Arthur E.: 66, 74
Barker, James: 24n, 94n, 95n, 153n
Bangs, Carl O.: 36n
Bartholomew, Ruth: 8, 34
Basil: 33, 189
Baynham, Sir Edmund: 39
Bede: 198
Bernard of Clairvaux: 36-37
Biel, Gabriel: 33
Boethius: 25-26
Bowra, C. M.: 42
Brisman, Leslie: 159
Browne, Sir Thomas: 42
Burroughs, Josephine: 28n
Calvin, John: 19, 27, 34, 35-36, 39
Calvinism: 7, 24n, 35-37, 42
Cambridge Platonists: 137, 154
Cambridge University: 47, 67
Caponigri, A. Robert: 30n
Capreolus, John: 33
Cassian, John: 24
Cassirer, Ernst: 25n, 27n
Catholicism (also Papistry): 7, 49, 96
Celestius: 20
Charles I: 38, 48, 73
Charles II: 73
Chosen People: 37, 42, 46, 48
Christian Liberty: 15, 77
Christianity: 17
Chrysostom, John: 33
Church Fathers: 9, 21, 23, 32-33, 35, 83-84, 95, 97, 128, 189
Circe: 55, 56
Civil War: 72

Clement of Alexandria: 147
Colet, John: 32
Commonwealth: 7, 38, 41, 73
Conklin, George: 42, 84, 83n, 122n
Council, Celestial: 101, 110, 117, 193
Council, Infernal: 108, 110, 141, 191
Counter-Reformation: 100n, 101
Crashaw, Richard: 100-102
Cromwell, Oliver: 71, 73
Cudworth, Ralph: 84, 128
Curry, Walter Clyde: 16n, 84n, 97, 123, 190-191
Cyprian: 24, 33
Cyril: 33
Damascene, John: 33
Damned Crew: 39, 43, 50, 57, 150, 171, 187
Dante: 198
Daphne: 61
De Deo creation: 122-123, 124
Democritus: 16
Devil's Crew, The: 39-40
Diekhoff, John S.: 163
Diodati, Charles: 41, 47
Dominicans: 16
Duns Scotus, John: 33
Durandus of Saint-Pourçain: 33
Eastland, Elizabeth: 8, 189n
Eleatics: 16
Election: 20, 24, 36
Elizabeth I: 37, 38, 42, 48
Empson, William: 87, 143-144
Epicurus: 16
Erasmus, Desiderius: 27, 32-34, 38-39, 135, 136, 153-154
Eusebius: 198
Evans, John M.: 8, 21n, 23n, 24n, 88n, 89n, 156, 189n
Ex Nihilo creation: 35, 83, 121, 124
Ficino, Marsilio: 27-31, 190
Fixler, Michael: 8
Florentine Academy: 32
Foreknowledge (see also Predestination): 25-27, 35, 81-82, 85-88, 90, 99-100, 108, 109, 110, 114-116, 148, 154, 166, 180

Fortunate Fall: 177, 188n
Foxe, John: 37, 42
Frye, Northrop: 107
Geiger, William: 12, 13
Gelli, Battista: 30n, 32
Giles of Rome: 33
Golden Age: 38, 42, 102
Grace: 16-28, 31, 33-37, 45-46, 55, 62, 79, 81, 98-99, 114, 148, 150-151, 153-154, 172, 175, 178, 181, 185, 188n, 189, 196
Gregory of Rimini: 33
Gregory the Great: 24
Gross, Barry: 8
Gunpowder Plot: 39, 47-48
Hakewill, George: 119
Hamilton, Gary: 8
Hanford, James H.: 100n
Hartwell, Kathleen Ellen: 88n, 189n
Hefele, Charles Joseph: 23n,
Herbert, Edward, Lord Herbert of Cherbury: 42
Hercules: 104
Hilary: 24, 33
Hobbes, Thomas: 128
Homer, Homeric: 82, 110
Homoousion: 95
Horace: 40
Hughes, Merritt Y.: 47n
Huizinga, Johann: 33n
Humanism: 7, 27, 28, 34, 40, 42, 189
Hunsaker, Orvil Glade: 24n
Hunter, William B., Jr.: 42, 97
Irenaeus: 152
Isidore of Seville: 24, 198
James I: 38, 39, 47-48, 49, 66
Jerome: 33, 198
Jesuits: 16
Jewel, John: 38, 42
Julian of Eclanum: 20
Jupiter: 26
Kelley, Maurice: 80n, 93, 96, 97, 121n, 126-127
King James Bible: 45, 46

King, Edward: 65, 66
Kristeller, Paul Oskar: 25n
Lactantius: 87-88, 153, 189
Laud, William: 38
Lawry, Jon S.: 65-66
Lever, Christopher: 149
Lewalski, Barbara K.: 96, 98
Lewis, C. S.: 138n, 144-146
Lieb, Michael: 32n
Limborch, Phillipus van: 96
Linacre, Thomas: 32
Luther, Martin: 19, 26, 32, 33, 37
Machiavelli, Niccolò; Machiavellian: 39, 47, 110
Manichaeus, Manichaeanism: 16, 17, 22, 27
Marshall, Peter: 38
Martz, Louis L.: 99, 100n
Mary I, 49
Masque: 54-63
Mazzeo, J. A.: 88n
McColley, Diane: 8, 98, 188n
McDill, Joseph Moody: 36n
Melancthon: 154
Metaphysical poetry: 49
Michael (Archangel): 178-187
Millenarianism: 42, 48
Miller, Milton: 189n
Milton, John
    "Apologus de Rustico et Hero": 46-47
    "At a Solemn Music": 51, 52-54, 56, 63-64
    "At a Vacation Exercise": 40-41
    "Elegy I": 47
    "Elegy VI": 41, 50
    "Il Penseroso": 7, 50-51
    "L'Allegro": 7, 40, 50-51
    "On the Death of a Fair Infant Dying of a Cough": 49, 68,
    "On the Morning of Christ's Nativity": 39-40, 49-50, 92-93, 100-103, 105-106
    "On the New Forcers of Conscience": 71
    "Passion, The": 98-99, 103-105
    "Psalm 114" (paraphrase): 44-46

"Psalm 136" (paraphrase): 47
"Sonnet VII": 51n
"Sonnet XI": 71
"Sonnet XII": 71
"Sonnet XIX": 71
"Sonnet XV": 71
"Sonnet XVI": 71, 76-77
"Sonnet XVII": 71
"Sonnet XVII": 71
"Upon the Circumcision": 51-52, 54, 98, 103, 105-106
An Apology against a Pamphlet Called "A Modest Confutation...": 72
Animadversions upon the Remonstrant's Defense against Smectymnuus: 72, 93
Areopagitica: 31, 42, 44, 73, 76, 87n, 155
Christian Doctrine, The: 80-81, 86-87, 89, 92-93, 96, 99, 119, 120, 122-123, 124, 126, 128-129, 135, 136, 152, 153, 154-155, 175, 195-197
Colasterion: 73
Comus: 7, 54-64, 65, 70
De Doctrina Christiana (see *Christian Doctrine, The*)
Defense of the English People: 74, 93
Divorce tracts: 74
Doctrine and Discipline of Divorce: 73
Eikonoclastes: 74
In Quintum Novembris: 47-48
Johannis Miltoni, Angli, pro populo Anglicano defensio contra Claudii Salmasii defensionem regiam (see *Defense of the English People*): 74
Johannis Miltoni, Angli, pro populo Anglicano defensio secunda (see *Second Defense of the English People*)
Johannis Miltoni, Angli, pro se Defensio: 74
Judgment of Martin Bucer: 73
Letter to a Friend, A: 74
Lycidas: 7, 49, 65-70
Nativity Ode (See "On the Morning of Christ's Nativity")
Naturam non Pati Senium: 119
Observations upon the Articles of Peace: 74
Of Education: 51n, 73, 79
Of Prelatical Episcopy: 72
Of Reformation Touching Church Discipline in England: 72, 74, 93

Paradise Lost: 13, 48, 52, 54, 57-58, 62, 64, 66, 70, 71, 76, 81, 83, 85-87, 88-90, 98, 99-100, 101, 107-113, 117-118, 120, 123, 124-126, 129-151, 152, 155-174, 175-190, 195-196, 198-199
Paradise Regained: 57, 62, 66, 92, 93, 98, 99, 107, 111-118, 139, 142-143, 149-150, 163
Present Means, and brief Delineation of a Free Commonwealth, The: 74
Ready and Easy Way to Establish a Free Commonwealth, The: 74
Reason of Church Government, The: 41, 72
Samson Agonistes: 62, 185-186
Second Defense of the English People: 8, 71-72, 74, 75, 76, 77
Tenure of Kings and Magistrates: 46, 73, 74, 77, 79
Tetrachordon: 71, 73
Treatise of Civil Power, A: 74, 75-76

Molinists: 16
More, Henry: 128, 154
More, Sir Thomas: 32
Moses: 41
Neoplatonism: 17, 28, 32, 42, 97, 154, 189
New Jerusalem, England as: 38
Nicaea, Council of: 95, 96, 97
Nicholson, Marjorie Hope: 154n
Orange, Council of (529 A.D.): 22
Origen: 32, 33, 84, 123, 124, 125-126, 128, 147, 153, 189
Original Sin: 18, 20, 23, 34, 36, 49
Orosius: 198
Otto of Freising: 198
Oxford English Dictionary: 45
Pallas: 29
Pandemonium: 82, 108, 109, 138, 141, 170
Panofsky, Erwin: 104
Pantheism: 128
Parliament: 38, 42
Patrides, C. A.: 96-97, 163, 198
Pauline skepticism: 20
Pelagius, Pelagianism: 19, 20-24, 31-33, 36
Philo: 97
Pico della Mirandola, Giovanni: 27-28, 30-32, 190
Plato: 41, 128
Platonism: 7, 28, 137

Plotinus: 97, 128
Pope: 47-49
Powell, Mary: 73
Predestination: 7, 18-25, 32, 34-36, 38, 39, 88, 127, 154-156
Prelapsarian state: 19, 36, 62, 133, 160, 177, 186
Presbyterianism: 44
Prometheus: 29
Prosper of Acquitaine: 88
Protestantism: 19, 37, 40, 48, 100n, 102
Psellus: 128
Puritanism: 7, 15
Pythagoreans: 16
Radzinowicz, Mary Ann Nevins: 8, 88, 177
Randall, John Herman, Jr.: 25n
Raphael (Angel): 86, 114, 125, 132-134, 157-160, 166, 174, 178, 183, 188, 190-193
Reformation: 32, 34, 38, 39-41, 72, 79, 100n
Regii Sanguinis Clamor Ad Coelum: 74
Revard, Stella: 8, 171
Richmond, Hugh M.: 144
Roberts, James D.: 85, 154n
Robins, Harry F.: 8, 84n, 124, 126
Saurat, Denis: 123, 126
Schaff, Philip: 19n
Scholasticism: 16, 25
Seaman, John E.: 8, 104n
Semi-Pelagianism: 23-24
Shaw, Catherine: 12
Shawcross, John T.: 32n
Sidney, Sir Philip: 32
Smectymnuus: 72
Socinianism: 7
Socrates: 16
Spenser, Edmund: 32
Sprott, S. E.: 39-40
Steadman, John M.: 12, 13, 16n, 138n, 154
Stein, Arnold: 163
Stoics: 16
Stoll, E. E.: 143, 144
Subordinationism: 7, 97, 98

Tatian: 189
Tertullian: 33, 97
Theophilus: 189
Theophylactus: 33
Thomism: 16
Tillyard, E. M. W.: 163
Tragedy: 41
Trinity, Trinitarianism: 92-93, 96, 100, 123, 196
Trinkhaus, Charles Edward: 25n, 27n
Tuve, Rosemond: 100n, 101n
Ulreich, John: 152-153
Uytenbogaert, Johannes: 15
Valla, Lorenzo: 25-28
Victor: 24
Vincent of Beauvais: 198
Vives, Juan Luis: 32
Waldock, A. J. A.: 163
Wallerstein, Ruth: 100n
Walton, Izaak: 42
War in Heaven: 50, 129-130, 140, 149
Westminster Confession (1647): 37
Whichcote: Benjamin: 84-85, 137, 154
Winter, Ernst F.: 16n, 27n, 33n, 34n, 35n, 135n, 153n
Woodhouse, A. S. P.: 8
Wycliffe, John: 27, 34
Zohar: 123

ABOUT THE AUTHOR

MICHAEL R. COLLINGS is an Emeritus Professor of English at Pepperdine University and the author of over thirty volumes of poetry, novels, short fiction, bibliography, and studies of writers including Stephen King, Dean R. Koontz, Piers Anthony, Brian W. Aldiss, and Orson Scott Card. Many of his books have been published by the Borgo Press Imprint of Wildside Press, his most recent being *The Art and Craft of Poetry*, the science-fiction novel, *Singer of Lies*, and a full-scale Renaissance Epic on the order of Milton's *Paradise Lost, The Nephiad: An Epic in XII Books*. He lives and works in Idaho.

www.ingramcontent.com/pod-product-compliance
Lightning Source LLC
LaVergne TN
LVHW041616070426
835507LV00008B/267